DARE TO TAKE CHARGE

DARE TO TAKE CHARGE

HOW TO LIVE YOUR LIFE
ON PURPOSE

JUDGE GLENDA
HATCHETT

CENTER
STREET

NEW YORK BOSTON NASHVILLE

Center Street
Hachette Book Group
237 Park Avenue
New York, NY 10017

www.centerstreet.com

Center Street is a division of Hachette Book Group, Inc.
The Center Street name and logo are trademarks of Hachette Book Group, Inc.

Printed in the United States of America

First Edition: September 2010

10 9 8 7 6 5 4 3 2 1

Library of Congress Cataloging-in-Publication Data

Hatchett, Glenda.
   Dare to take charge : how to live your life on purpose / by Glenda Hatchett.
      p. cm.
   ISBN 978-1-59995-330-4
   1. Goal (Psychology)   2. Success.   3. Self-realization.   I. Title.

   BF505.G6H38 2010
   650.1—dc22

                                                            2009051955

To my Mother,
Clemmie Elizabeth Barnes Hatchett,
upon whose strong, courageous,
and resourceful shoulders I stand.
Thank you for challenging me
to dare and to dream by your bold example.

With love, deep respect, and appreciation,

Contents

Introduction

The pages you hold in your hand may surprise you. *Dare to Take Charge* is designed to help you turn a corner in your life. It will challenge you to change. It will make you question how you handle your life and help you start doing just one thing every day to better your circumstances, to reach for your dreams. *Dare to Take Charge* will challenge you to make *daring* a part of how you deal with changing your life for the better.

Changing our lives does take daring. If you ask anyone whom you consider a success, I guarantee you will find that achievement requires that you learn to practice courage in your daily life. Being brave is all about daring—to take action, to define your own goals, to try new things and tread unfamiliar ground, to never give up. Daring will bring your dreams back into focus. I challenge you to try. I dare you to take charge of your own accomplishments, from the smallest step forward to the largest of victories. If you dare, then doors will open. But you also need to start planning—now—what you will do when those possibilities present themselves. *Dare to Take Charge* is 100 percent about creating, accessing, and being ready for possibilities when they arrive.

Times get tough when our hopes seem out of reach. When what we want to achieve seems inaccessible, we often worry and stop trying. But our dreams and desires only become hard to reach when we fail to purposefully devote ourselves to achieving them. Living life to the fullest takes both nerve and optimism. That's why in each chapter of this book, I dare you to dream, to achieve, to plan, to let go of what you don't need, and to carefully define and pursue your purpose. Crossing over to a path that suits your passions and your dreams is possible, if you live your life on purpose. In this book, I dare you to reach for opportunity, time and time again. I want you to challenge yourself too. Every gain in this world comes from reaching, stretching, trying. *Dare to Take Charge* seeks to motivate you to take these actions in your own life.

Dare to Take Charge presents proven strategies for confronting the challenges we face in life. It focuses on learning to subdue the struggles that can delay or defeat us. *Dare to Take Charge* challenges you, and dares you, to keep working toward your dreams. If we use our lives to work toward our dreams, then our dreams will be much more likely to become our realities.

How to Use This Book

Dare to Take Charge is organized by life lessons—those I have learned from my own experience and those I have been party to by intervening in the crises that came to my courtroom. Life is a stern yet loving teacher. If we get the message, life supports us. If we stay confused, we have to live through the chaos confusion causes.

Although you will learn much about me and my story, this book is not a memoir. My goal in sharing my story and the stories of others is to give you an example. But the goal of this book is to give you tools you can use and principles you can practice that will allow you to march resolutely in the direction of *your* dreams. The life lessons revealed in these chapters are chosen because they are abundantly clear. You may find your story in these pages. You may find exactly your worries. You will find many steps you can take to move yourself forward, based on how you see your purpose in this life. Life lessons require problem-solving, and you will read of many problems being solved in these pages. Even if the examples I give don't match your situation exactly, you will still learn lessons that will help you deal with whatever you are facing. This book will help you take charge of your own problem-solving.

If you start right away, you put yourself immediately on the path toward greater fulfillment in life. If you practice these principles, if you dare to take charge, you really will change how you handle your choices. You will give yourself the opportunity to get and remain on the path toward making your dreams your reality. You can begin to make different choices so that you can respond to obstacles without letting them stop your progress.

Take the time you need to read and practice what you discover in this book. If you need to read and process slowly, you are welcome to. If you're a fast worker, a go-getter, then read, plan, and take action at the speed your life permits. If you want to focus on one life lesson each week, then do. Feel free to take the sections more slowly. Take charge of your own use of the lessons of a lifetime. At whatever speed you use this book, I have worked to introduce you to new concepts that will move you from crisis to creativity, that will take you from pain to purpose.

As you read, you may find that you want to return again and again to some principles. Of course, I am going to encourage you to do just that. Mark the sections that present ideas that feel like news. Also mark the sections that articulate struggles you recognize. Write notes in the margins—it's your book. Make this a well-worn manual. Return to the sections you've marked and practice until the change comes naturally. Use this information in a way that really helps *you*.

Did you know you've already taken two steps toward your positive future? First, you chose to buy this book. And then you chose to pick it up and start reading. As you read the book more deeply, your efforts will increase. Every day, take one step, however small. To help you do this, at the end of each chapter you'll find one thing to do that day to get you started. But after you've read and understood the full range of the life lessons, your work begins in earnest. You'll find a summary of the ideas and goals to work toward in the "Dare To" section that concludes each chapter. Be conscious. Be intentional. Be daring. Practice all the listed efforts. Identify the principles you need the most, and begin to work on each lesson specifically.

There is no one way to practice these principles, just as there is no one path to success. You do not have to practice the principles in order, but you do have to practice *all* the principles. What success means for you is up to you to define. *Starting right away is the one requirement.* Promise yourself, as you begin this journey, that you *will* pursue your destiny. Take one action, every day, from now on. Give yourself the gift of taking charge of your own life.

If you use this book, if you practice these principles, if you dare to take charge, you *will* feel more courage. You will have more knowledge, and you will be more energized to reach for what you dream.

My Share of Hard Times

Many of you know me from my TV show, *Judge Hatchett.* My seasons in a television courtroom and my years as a juvenile court judge have allowed me to witness the life experiences and appreciate the lessons learned by so many people. Children, women, and men came into my courtroom hurting, worried, outraged, or lost. My job was to sort through the many crises and dilemmas. I looked at every situation, every child, every parent, every person—and tried to figure out how to inject possibility into a painful situation.

In my work as a judge and in my life as a woman and as a single mother, I have encountered, directly or indirectly, almost every kind of life challenge imaginable. I've leapt over many hurdles in my life, sometimes without knowing whether I would make it. On occasion, I have tripped, and I have fallen. I've helped others surmount challenges in their own lives. I've done a lot of work, a lot of problem-solving and thinking about what principles we need to practice not just to survive, but to thrive.

Almost daily as a judge, I see people wrestling with their worries, their fears, and their limitations. Some of these battles are rough, sometimes tragic, sometimes extreme. I advise parents, young people, and relatives who are struggling to survive on how to solve family problems, how to improve or save their own lives or the lives of relatives who have strayed from the path. I have also worked with people unrelated to each other who have entered into agreements or made deals that have not turned out the way either party wanted and ended up in court. I have intervened in many family dramas, on television and in life.

As I mentioned, there are stories of my life and the lives of others included throughout this book. For those of you who have watched my courtroom show, there will be people and stories you recognize. I have used the real names of some of the people who have appeared in my courtroom on television. For those who have not appeared on television, I have changed their names, so that we all can learn from their stories.

None of us controls *all* of what we encounter. For example, none of us is responsible for how we start out in life. Some writers call this "the accident of birth." However, each one of us *can* control how we end up. How and where we finish in life depends on how we handle what we're faced with along the way. How we respond to problems and challenges often makes the difference between winning and losing, between winning and worrying, between winning and giving up. Every one of us faces some disappointments in life, at some time. All of us know firsthand about discouragement. In these circumstances, the clearest advice I can give is: *Dare to dream.*

The stories you read in this book will help you understand and practice taking charge of your life. If you follow the strategies you read in these chapters, you will also see that your future is yours to shape.

The Focus Is on You

In this book, the focus is on *you.* On helping you win, on helping you achieve the goals you define, on helping you take charge to create the forever that burns in your heart. Your dreams are your vision of the future. That future waits—patiently or impatiently—for your attention, for your efforts, for your dedication to making a reality of the dreams that live on in your mind. Our responses to our struggles, combined with the positive actions that we initiate, can help us dare to hold on to our dreams.

People have intentions and make plans all the time that do not result in their desired outcomes. This is the birthplace of struggle: when our intentions fail to produce the results we seek. We feel conflict in our lives when our desires are not in sync with our actions. The life lessons and exercises in this book will challenge you to bring your actions and your dreams more in line.

Dare to Take Charge is written to teach you, or to remind you, that your future is yours to shape. You *can* overcome tough times. My strategy of daring has worked for me and countless others, time and again. If you dare to commit to what you're doing, although you may stumble or falter, you will not fail. If you dare to get up and try again, you will not fail. If you dare to honor your instincts and desires, you will not fail. If you dream, and make pursuing your dreams a priority, you will gain much more of the life you desire.

If you are looking for an easy way out, this is not the book for you. If you want to change your life without working, without learning new skills, this is not the book for you. But if you understand that persistence and a willingness to try again can move you away from a state of crisis and despair, then you will find tools in this book that will inspire you and equip you to create the life you want.

I have written this book out of love and hope, and out of a compelling need to share many of the lessons I've learned from the many people I've encountered. I want the best for you, which means for you to treat your dreams with care. You can retrain yourself: you can find the time to achieve more. You can live better, if you choose, you can pursue the urgings of your heart and your mind. I have done this; I have encouraged others, and watched them do the same. By all means, *Dare to Take Charge*. Turn the page.

DARE TO TAKE CHARGE

One

How Dare You Not?

We all have our touchstones—mothers, fathers, aunts, uncles, teachers, mentors, friends—who have pierced through a fog we were in at one time or another and set us back on our path. We all have people we can quote: "My mother used to say," "My father told me," "My teacher always said." I happen to have many supporters, teachers, advisers, and friends—you will meet some of them in the pages that follow. I'd like to start by introducing you to my kind and wise Aunt Frances.

My Aunt Frances was a pillar in our family. She was my grandmother's sister, and so all the time I knew her she was an older woman, a wise elder. She had lived her life with dignity and finished her professional life with pride. She was someone who had thrived in life, and who continued to live as an example in her old age. Aunt Frances was also a devout Christian—very strict, but loving and warm. She had seen the worst days of the segregated South. Before she retired, she lovingly labored for more than forty years as a schoolteacher—making half the salary of her white counterparts. I never heard her complain about that gross injustice. She had lived through enormous challenges, and she spoke eloquently through her words and deeds.

At a time in my life when I felt particularly discouraged, I went to see my Aunt Frances, and her advice so changed me that the moment is emblazoned on my consciousness, and my meeting with her remains a significant moment in my life story. In fact, Aunt Frances's response to me and advice to me was so bold and so perceptive that she offered me something that I have continued to use. I share Aunt Frances's advice as I advise others and as I make my way through the high and low points of my life.

When I began my professional life, I chose to go to law school. Like many others, I expected that the law would help me to achieve and contribute to bettering my life, my community, my culture, and my country. I started law school with eager anticipation and very high hopes.

My great expectations were short-lived. I soon faced challenges I had not expected. During my first year in law school, I became over-whelmed. I felt like I had far too much on my plate. I worked full-time as the assistant to the dean for women to pay my tuition, and was also the director of the women's residential complex. Both of these were positions for which I had to be alert and responsible for the welfare of others. I found myself sleep-deprived, overworked, and stressed out. The pressure of my studies and the tremendous responsibility of working my way through school caused me to wonder what I had been thinking. I started to wonder about the choice I had made.

In spite of my intentions, I hated law school. I had only just started, but I was really questioning why I went in the first place. I needed advice, I needed sympathy, I needed affection. I knew where to go. So on a cool fall day in Atlanta, I shut my books and drove to see my Aunt Frances at her house on Bon Air.

We Are All Uniquely Situated

On the drive, I had time to consider my situation. Although I'd never been a quitter, I was seriously thinking about quitting. I wasn't sure exactly what I'd say to Aunt Frances about all this, but I was confident that seeing her, and removing myself from the source of my stress, would help me clear my head.

Everything in Aunt Frances's house was meticulously neat and traditional. She greeted me as she always did, with the warm, loving hug I was craving. Aunt Frances was generous with her life and her affection. She told me I needed "meat on my bones," and invited me into her kitchen to eat. Looking deeply into my eyes, she could tell right away I was troubled.

Aunt Frances kept the same old sofa for my entire life. I curled up on that sofa, and since Aunt Frances could see that my heart was heavy, she asked me what was wrong. I was so stressed, I didn't need much prompting. I went on and on about how absolutely miserable I was in law school. Aunt Frances sat and listened. I moaned and whined about how terrible law school was, until Aunt Frances finally stopped me and asked just one question.

"Do you want to be a lawyer?"

I nodded, not even speaking aloud.

Then Aunt Frances said words that changed my life forever.

"Baby, if it were easy, everybody and their mama would be able do what you're trying to do," she said. "But it isn't easy, and you've been uniquely situated and blessed with the gifts to be able to do what you set out to do."

My Aunt Frances held my gaze as tears rolled down my face. I thought, *Aunt Frances has seen the worst of times. She has been a survivor and has been victorious with a mere fraction of my opportunities. Here I am, in law school. I didn't have to fight or march or file suit to get in. I am in law school, which is where I said I wanted to be. Aunt Frances has struggled more than I have ever had to, more than I could ever imagine. How dare I complain?*

Before me sat one of my sheroes, concerned about me. My Aunt Frances had done more with less. Her years of unwavering dedication, and her now unwavering gaze, caused me to look at the "me she must see." I became very uncomfortable with myself, and particularly with my whining. *How dare I moan and groan about opportunities Aunt Frances could never have dreamed of? Aunt Frances expects me to see grace in my life, that I am able to attend law school at all.*

Aunt Frances was very patient with me, and I imagine she could see my thoughts shifting.

How dare I not claim my dream and my destiny? How dare I falter? How dare I not march forward with all the purpose and passion I can muster? How dare I not stand up, restore my faith, and go on ahead? Who ever told me that this road would be easy?

Get Up

I got up off Aunt Frances's sofa standing taller. She taught me as much with her generous listening, her plain questioning, and her patient waiting as she did with the statement she made. Of course, I had always made choices that not everybody was making. All my life, I've chosen to do things that aren't necessarily easy. The roads I traveled have been easier, certainly, than the work that my parents and their parents and the heroes—and sheroes—of my Aunt Frances's generation had to do. But the thought that I should expect anything but hard work was absurd. The idea that I should moan and groan, whine and complain—how dare I? I don't know what I was thinking. But sitting with my Aunt

Frances that afternoon reminded me of the stock I had come from. Her very presence caused me to remember to stand up and get strong.

I made up my mind, from that day forward, that as I approached the important things in my life, I would keep my nerve and face my challenges. Strength, consistency, determination, integrity, purpose—these are all the values Aunt Frances and my grandparents and my parents lived by. These are the principles that helped keep them on the high road.

I had opportunities to live out my passion and my choices. I needed to do all I could to match my actions to my intentions, and no less. I needed to persist until I created the outcomes I was looking for. I needed to remain open to the possibilities that came along with the goals I set, and the dreams I reached for. I needed to refuse to be derailed by the pitfalls.

That important talk with Aunt Frances, at the very beginning of my career as a law student, helped me understand what to do, in every instance, when I found myself knocked down. It's as simple as this:

Dare to get up.

I have to thank Aunt Frances for being so direct and so expectant— both with her question and with her gaze—to help me shake myself out of my state of self-pity. I had decided that I was going to have a pity party, and I had begun, with myself as the only guest. I don't think I ever expected Aunt Frances to join me. Our parents and our foreparents tended not to pity themselves. But Aunt Frances was remarkably plain and expectant. Her response to me was daring and insistent, in as quiet a tone as possible.

Sitting before her suggested much more than words needed to express. No one was going to finish law school for me. Fewer doors were going to open to me if I failed to finish law school. And then would I whine about what I couldn't do, if I had chosen to become a law school dropout?

The answer to this question does not matter. I decided that I had to persist. I had to ask myself, a thousand times if necessary: *How can I not take the best advantage of the opportunity before me? How can I not recognize that my dreams are my soul's gift to my life?*

I did not leave Aunt Frances, go back to law school, and find that all my problems were magically solved. Finishing law school did not get easier. But my determination swallowed up my uncertainty. I faced the same daily struggle and I leaned into the same alienating experience that had driven me to Aunt Frances in the first place.

But here I am today, many years and many doorways after almost quitting law school. I daresay, as a judge, that the law has been essential to my success. Truthfully, my success in life would depend on my accepting this: I could not abandon my goals. I could not discount my dreams. I could not sell my hopes short. I could not and would not fail.

You Too Have to Dare

And so this is what I say to you. You too have to dare. Daring is an underrated character trait. In order to achieve almost anything of importance, we have to find the nerve, the audacity; we have to be daring.

To dare is a verb that has two meanings. When we do something unusual, significant, or in some way remarkable, we dare, and are generally commended. We have the hope to dream, we have the courage to try, we insist on being persistent, we have the will to become all that we are able.

The second meaning relates mostly to a spirit of questioning. How dare you? How dare I? How dare I not do what I know I need to do? How dare you not do all that you are able? Rather than standing up to the doubts of the world, sometimes we need to stand up to ourselves, to our own doubts, reluctance, or excuses. Sometimes we need to challenge ourselves.

Once I realized how much I had learned about life—through my own experiences, and through my work with the many troubled and triumphant people and families who came through my courtrooms—my knowledge begged the question: How dare I not make an effort to share these stories? How dare I not see the importance of the understanding I have gained from having experience with family after family, crisis after crisis, victory after effort, triumph after intervention?

I dare you to invoke your God-given spirit. I dare you to tell yourself the truth. I dare you to recapture dreams you may have let go, and I dare you to help your children get closer to their dreams—now. I dare you to learn from the mistakes of others. I dare you to examine your heart.

I want you to realize that living out your full potential is not just possible, not just in your best interest, but also is what your family and your community and your spirit need from you. I want to help you reach your full potential because without working toward living the best life we can, we are not honoring our gifts or our time on this earth.

Any one of us can choose not to do our very best. But that's when I ask the question: *How dare you not?*

Dare to support your own goals, to invest in yourself, to protect your relationships, to let go of the tendency to pity yourself in times of struggle. You have to face what you lack, and you have to figure out how to answer that lack with focus and directed energy. You have to stop struggling and start succeeding; you have to find out how others have succeeded at what you want to do. You have to learn from their models of success. You have to plow through the doldrums, and plow through your fears.

Just as Aunt Frances advised me, you too have to claim and embrace the wonderful blessings in your life. You have to persist, try again, try another way. You have to knock harder on the door, if that's what it takes to be heard. You have to stand up and go forward. You have to bring your dreams into focus.

No one knows your intentions like you do. No one feels the fire of your desires like you do. No one can or will accomplish what you want to achieve—except you.

We all could use more daring in our lives. We could stretch ourselves and find out how to start that business, how to get into that training program, how to get through law school, how to become an architect. We can do the work to teach our children about money, about faith, about self-respect and positive choices. We can step out of our comfort zone and do what we dream of, and make new priorities based on what we've been too afraid or too worried to tackle up to now.

Daring is the secret.

I invite you to move yourself boldly forward on the road you are traveling in this life. Go forward, with me, from my Aunt Frances's patient gaze. Know that you can get past difficult times, and that when you achieve your dream, you will look back and realize it was worth the struggle.

Today:

What is the one thing that you have always wanted to do in your life and have not yet done? Take time now to write down what you haven't done, and then write down why you haven't done it. What's holding you back? How dare you not follow through on your honest ambitions? Do you dare not try?

Dare To...

Do what you dream of doing.

- Work toward the grace of fulfillment.
- Be clear with yourself about what your life requires or demands of you.

Live out your gifts.

- Depend on, and act on, the grace of God within you.
- Increase the amount of time you spend doing what you're good at.

Reach.

- Take the high road.
- Expect more of yourself.

Two

Bridging the Dream Gap

When was the last time you checked in with your dreams? What is it that you want more than anything? What do you want to achieve in your lifetime? When you imagine yourself as successful, accomplished, joyful— what does that look like? To *view* your dreams is important: the dreams we actually *see* are the goals we can attain. *Imagine a different future.* Ask yourself, really, what is your dream for your life? The sky is the limit. What would you do, if you dared, that you have not yet done? Are you able to articulate your dream without struggling? Is your dream top of mind?

Dr. Peter Singleton

Growing up, I had a play big brother. He was not actually related to me, but I admired and cherished him as a "big brother." He grew into an amazing man, and although he passed on a few years ago, he still inspires me as a phenomenal human being—a gifted doctor, humanitarian, and man of the world.

Pete spoke more than a dozen different languages and dialects. When I spoke in tribute to him, I was able to recount such wonderful stories, but the one that really rang out from my heart was about his being my role model, a part of my village, a great achiever within my reach.

For as long as I can remember, whenever anyone asked Pete what he wanted to be when he grew up, without hesitation he boldly responded—a doctor. His parents believed he would become a doctor. My parents would introduce Pete as "the future doctor." Dad called him Dr. Singleton long before he finished medical school. We all believed that being a doctor was Pete's future.

He did become a doctor, and what a doctor he became! Before he retired from the military, he provided medical care throughout the world. When his life ended so prematurely, he was serving with distinction on the faculty of Stanford University's medical school. Peter Singleton's dream became his reality, and *the world was better because he claimed his dream*.

Can you find the Peter Singleton in you? If you were going to be single-minded about achieving one goal in your life, what would that goal be? In order to claim it, you have to first name it.

Do you dream of going back to school now—maybe you are in your fifties, and your children are all grown? Have you always dreamed of getting your degree in art history? Did you want to be a college professor? Do you dream of living debt-free? Perhaps you dream of owning and restoring a vintage car, or learning to play golf, or retiring before you are sixty? Do you dream of quitting the job that you hate and starting your own business? Perhaps you'd like to create a business that your children and grandchildren will own? Do you dream of learning to speak Spanish fluently, or perhaps you dream of being a vice president in your company? Do you want to travel around the world, or do you dream of being elected to the United States Congress? Do you dream of being happily married? Perhaps you dream of being an award-winning novelist or winning an Oscar as an actor? Do you dream of saving enough money to buy a home? Do you dream of being independently wealthy? Do you dream of living a life free of your addiction? Whichever dream you define, make that dream your number one goal.

Dreams give us incentive and keep us excited about life. Dreams help us to live life on purpose. This is important to remember at all stages of our lives. Just as Pete's parents supported his dream to be a doctor, you should encourage the children in your life to dream bold dreams. Click on the Dreams Campaign tab at ParentpowerNow.com.

Stop right here, right now, and write down what you dream of accomplishing for yourself. Be bold and intentional. Be daring. You have all the choices in the world. Do not go any further until you have recorded at least one dream you have. If you need to stop and think, then by all means, stop and think. But do yourself a great favor, give yourself a great gift and identify a dream. Identify a dream that if it came true, you'd feel happy, and blissful, and blessed. Stop. Think. Write.

This is what I dream of when there are no limits.

_____

_____

_____

_____

_____

                                    Your Signature

When you have stated your dream and written it clearly, please sign your name on the signature line.

Let knowing that you have a dream begin to move you to think about how to attain it. Think about your notation often, and ask yourself, *Am I currently on the path toward attaining my dream? Am I in pursuit of my dream, right now?*

Just because we're adults doesn't mean we can stop dreaming. Dreams are our divine hookup. Dreams are our road map, showing us the way to our future. If we will do ourselves the favor of taking the journey, making the trip, we can call our dreams our destination. Our dreams are our specific view of our own future.

Dreams Are Realities Every Day

Are your fantasies recent? Maybe there's something you've always wanted to accomplish, a person you've imagined being since you were a child, an idea you've put to the side as "real life" got in the way. Have you retired your dreams to the back of your mind and left them there? Are your dreams collecting dust? Are your dreams patiently (or impatiently) waiting for your attention?

Langston Hughes famously wrote this question in "Dream Deferred," a poem. It is perhaps one of his most famous poems, which has been used widely and provocatively to explain or examine the very human condition of letting our dreams take a backseat to the demands of our lives.

In it Hughes lists the possibilities for what we face when we do not attend to our dreams. While his descriptions seem poetic, none of them are appealing, as he suggests an unattended dream might shrivel up like a raisin or fester like an unattended sore. Even when he uses a positive description, comparing a dream to a "syrupy sweet," the option has a negative, over-sugared quality. Hughes's diverse description in this brief poem suggests many consequences. He concludes that when we ignore our dreams, when we defer them, when we put them off or push them to the side, they can be a heavy load—a burden. They might even explode.

Taking charge of your life means that you will realize and honor the important role big goals play in keeping you alive and vibrant. That dreams we don't attend to have the potential to weigh us down, or to explode within us, is a testament to how important they are. Dreams course through us like blood through our systems. Dreams contribute to life the same way that hours contribute to making seasons. Even if you are just dragging your dreams behind you, I guarantee you that you are still holding on to some little hope for realizing what you've always wanted to be or do. And there's something else that's true: even if you don't achieve your dream, if you are intentional, you will either accomplish much of what you intend to or you will discover a passion in yourself for some new interest you find on the way. I challenge you to put your dreams in their rightful place in your life: front and center.

Get in touch with your dreams again. Check in with dreams you haven't seen, spoken of, or acted on lately. Remind yourself of what you're actually doing: remind yourself that every day, you rise up and you go forward and do what you plan to do. You may not do all of what you plan to do, and you may not plan to do what you dream. But every day you live, you rise from slumber and you take step after step, and those steps are actions you *decide to take.* Congratulate yourself for living your life with energy and intention. I certainly congratulate you. Now I want to encourage you to start moving your actions closer to the actions that your dreams would have you take.

Do your daily efforts bear some relationship to your dreams? Are you applying your time and energy to move yourself toward what you, in your heart, really want to be doing? When you arrange your actions and your life so that you are moving in the direction of your dreams, you *will* experience joy. Are you experiencing joy in your life? Joy in life is your birthright. Every human being is able to make choices about what they will do, where they will go, what activities they will turn their attention to. Are you exercising your choices fully? Are you making choices that relate to your dreams?

Maybe you are among the many who have deferred your dreams. Maybe your dreams are sleeping. It's time for a new day. Are you ready to make a change? Are you ready to experience the joy of matching how you spend your days with how you dream your dreams?

Write five actions, however small, that you could take in the next five days to move you toward your stated dream. Take five actions. And then name five more. Take those five actions, and then name five more. Keep taking action: small actions are fine. Eventually you will take bigger, broader action, because you will be both motivated and pleased by what you have accomplished with the small actions you've taken.

Surely you have heard others refer to a dream or a goal having no meaning without a schedule; all goals need to have time allocated to address them or there is a great risk that these goals will not be accomplished. Similarly, realizing a dream requires that we take action toward achieving it in our everyday lives. And this is why I say: *Dreams are realities every day.*

If you work toward your dreams in addition to what you do every day, then you will be constantly inching closer to achieving them. You greatly reduce the risk of being loaded down with dusty dreams, of being burdened by the constant worry over what you haven't done. If you are always doing something toward achieving your goals, then you move your dream from a wish to a reality. The big picture will come ever closer to you.

You know by now that the theme of this book is daring. To take charge of your life, you have to dare to be in charge. You have to dare to take action. You have to dare to respond to the whispers of your soul and the stirrings of your heart. The idea that dreams are realities every day relates explicitly to the dare principle.

Dreams
Are
Realities
Every day

Attend to your dreams as you DARE to take charge. Your dreams will lead you to the life you are destined to have. Your dreams are seeds that come straight from your spirit. Your job in this life is to nurture your dreams and to help them grow. If you help your dreams grow, your dreams will help you go—go forward, go happily, go with hope, go with intention, go with consciousness, go with God.

Reaching for our dreams can take great effort. The effort required to achieve what we dream of is exactly why so many people quit working toward their dreams. Yes, achieving them takes diligence, persistence, and insistence. But all of life requires work. No matter what we choose to do in life, we have to work to stay alive. Why not work toward your heart's desires? Why not seek joy?

When we stop dreaming, we stop thinking about the future. When we stop thinking about the future, we stop living our lives to the fullest.

Our dreams define the direction we should go in. By making the effort to name our dreams, and by working to realize them, we take the practical step *of laying claim to our tomorrows.*

A Dream with Your Name on It

There is a dream with your name on it. You know, clearly, what that dream is. Nobody can see what we dream of better than we can. No one else can claim our dreams, either. Your dreams are *your* destiny, if you are willing to reach for them. *We put our handprint on the future by pursuing our dreams.*

None of us should be satisfied unless we are shaping our lives to move us toward our dreams. I could argue pretty safely, I think, that if we are not shaping our lives so that we are moving toward our dreams, we probably are dissatisfied. We might even be generally sad.

Look at the clock or your watch—what time is it? What time are you reading this? Is it 11:59 a.m. or p.m.? Is it 5:15 in the morning? Is it 7:30 in the evening, or 10:00 at night? Whatever time of day or night, it is *right now*; you are on the precipice of your future. Your future is not owned by your past. Your future is owned by your energy and your choices.

Every one of us realizes, and needs to remember, that our lives are, in some measure, ours to shape. One of our biggest decisions is whether we plan to stay stuck in the past or whether we will choose an alternative future. All too often, people lock themselves in vicious, repetitive cycles. You are only destined to repeat patterns that you choose to repeat. Breaking patterns is hard work, but life is hard work. You can break the patterns that rob you of your dreams and that rob you of your joy.

Do something, today, to help bring your dream into the reality of your life. By taking action that leads you toward your dream, you will do yourself an enormous service. You will begin to break the pattern that keeps you from dreaming, that keeps you from behaving as if your dreams are within your reach.

Your dreams, with your effort, can become your reality.

The most important question is, what are you doing today to move closer to those dreams? For example, if you dream of living debt-free, then you have to resolve today to live on a budget, cut up all your credit cards except the one that you use only for emergencies, and systematically work your way out of debt. What can you do starting today? This is the key question.

Start now. Do something, however small, every day. *Dreams are realities every day.* Remember, this means that if you move actions related to your dreams into your daily reality, you are buying yourself engagement, satisfaction, a direction in life. By pursuing your dreams, step by step, you are daring to take charge of your life.

At the beginning of the chapter, I asked you to write down a dream. This one dream is a starting point. But I want you to take even more time. Think about other dreams you've had in your life, as you go through the next twelve or twenty-four hours. Find some quiet time. Make a list of the dreams you think of, or that you've had in the past. Remember. Brainstorm. You're now on the path toward taking charge of your life. All the dreams you have help to shape what you will do. What dreams will you pursue?

Today:

Answer this question: What is the boldest dream you dare to dream for your life? Write it down in clear terms and post it where you can see it every day.

Dare To...

Bring your dreams into your daily reality.

- Start every day with a clear idea of what you can do, this day, to work toward a dream that you value.
- Expect every day to be a day in which you move closer to your dream.
- Be willing to experience the joy and satisfaction that come from involving your motivations and your personality in the actions you take on a daily basis.

Keep your dreams a high priority.

- Realize and remember that if you don't make a priority of your dreams, then you are not making a priority of yourself.
- Understand that no one is going to pursue your dreams for you.
- Know that there are dreams with your name on them: your dreams await you.

Take charge.

- Be aware that your dreams point the way to your future.
- Do the work that is required to live the life you dream of.
- Make yourself the person of your dreams.

Three

Hope and Joy

Some people are born, it seems, knowing the formula that permits them to wake up each morning certain that the new day will dawn better and brighter than the last. Others struggle to get the right balance of hope and high expectation in their lives—adding or subtracting strategies, techniques, new efforts. Living hopefully and optimistically is a goal of almost every person, whether they are successful or still trying to be successful. We all have to test which actions or strategies will work to help us achieve our goals.

Life without optimism can turn from dream to nightmare, and can make us wonder whether what we are experiencing is all there is to life. *Is this what I'm living for? Is this all there is?* Trust in the future and trust in the spiritual goodness of others is also important to have. The ability to know joy, to create joy, and to *re*create joy are essential skills to having a good life. We all need energy enough to try and try again. I live my days with the strong opinion that hope and optimism are basic necessities for a life well lived. Without the optimistic belief that the best days are yet to come, I think it's hard to keep going, to keep strategizing, and to overcome setbacks. Without being able to observe our joys, we simply cannot achieve the goals we set. Goals are, by definition, conceived in joy. Failures are obstacles that can teach us, but if we stare at our failures too long, they block us from joy, which in turn blocks us from success.

Count It All Joy

When I was young, my grandmother used to quote Scripture and say, "Count it all joy." As I grew up, this Bible verse (James 1:2) did not resonate all that well with me, because life does have its struggles and hurts. But the verse goes on to reference trials in life, and I've come to understand that the idea is that even in the pain of life there is joy to be found.

When I went through the acute experience of the pain of my father's passing, my grandmother's voice spoke to me. "Count it all joy" came to mind. Although I welcome the soothing and calming power of my grandmother's wisdom whenever I hear her voice, my grief definitely worried and weakened my usual sense of optimism and strength. In reality, however, I did finally hear through the message.

My father, who was my great hero, had spent much of his life, and all of mine, loving, teaching, and caring for me as a devoted parent. He raised me, he protected me, and he gave me great courage. He also gave me tremendous understanding: of compassion, perseverance, patience, and understanding. To know my father had been a joy—a very long-term and inspiring presence of joy in my life. So, yes, although his passing brought forth a time of great heaviness in my heart, my heart also beats in part because of him. I knew love because of him. I had a great hero because of him. All of this is joy.

For some folks, hope and optimism are just not part of the way they learned to think, or choose to think. Hope is a choice, a very powerful choice. Hope can give us strength, and can change our expectations about how a situation will turn out. People who are both hopeful and faithful have the power to create joy in their lives. My experience of the power of hope and optimism keeps me encouraging others to live on the side of optimism.

When all is said and done, I am relentlessly hopeful as a person and as a professional. In order to do the sometimes distressing work I do, I have to be optimistic. I have to look at every situation and ask myself repeatedly and sincerely, *How can I help? What is the potential for good here?*

Good is the only foundation worth building on. Two wrongs don't make a right, they just make more wrong. Being able to look at situations hopefully, to consider that there has to be something good I can raise up, is what enables me to reach ever higher. I can't say I know when I learned this lesson, but I can say that I have taken the search for hope completely and totally to heart. I look for how I can be hopeful. And what a blessing that has been.

Let me be clear. It's not that every day I live is better than the day before. But what inspires and centers me is my fundamental belief that the days to come will bring greater blessings and new successes. Expecting and working toward a better future is the basic definition of optimism.

I was genetically hard-wired to embrace the gospel of *the best is yet to come*. This comes from my parents, who saw plenty that might have convinced them otherwise, but they held tight to the ideal. They passed this spirit of optimism and expectation to my brothers and me. This spirit of hope has been critical to my survival and success. The spirit of hope is necessary to experience joy in any measure.

Optimism isn't automatic, and holding on to hope can be challenging. I see other people who seem to be more able (than me) to paint their lives the color of hope using big, sweeping brushstrokes—no matter how rough the going.

The absence of hope can rob us of our joy. Hope is a protective feeling that inoculates the spirit and keeps despair from settling in and taking root. When we can remain hopeful, or when we've learned to reset ourselves and restore our feelings of optimism after setbacks, then we create openings in our lives for joy to enter and cheer us.

We tend to focus on what hurts us in our lives. We are all able to recount or revisit pain we've felt far longer and far more easily than we are able to recall our joys. This tendency—to overlook the good and focus on the bad—causes us to hang our heads and expect the worst. Philosophers and psychologists and successful men and women have argued for decades that what we expect, we get.

Some of you may know one of Henry Ford's most famous quotations: "If you think you can do a thing or think you can't do a thing, you're right." Our interpretations of events, and our responses to them, become the ideas that define us and that either motivate or constrain us. In time, our ideas and our interpretations become our beliefs. If we focus on the negative, then we believe what we think. If we focus on the positive, then we believe what we think.

Failing to observe positive aspects in life causes us to see every half-full glass as half empty. Events or situations, however small, that we would otherwise celebrate are lost to us. We lose the potential of applauding ourselves. We turn into people who only see our trials and failures. We become people who "think we can't."

Some of us have heard or may remember the spiritual "Joy Comes in the Morning." The old song serves to remind us that no pain or sadness lasts forever, and that eventually there is always a new dawn. If you wait, a new day will come. Just as we expect morning to come, we should also rest ourselves, reset ourselves, and expect joy to grace our lives.

Your Joy Journal

I encourage you to develop a brand-new habit. Seek joy. Pursue joy. Make a note of the joy you find. Try taking joy notes for twenty-one days. Give yourself three good weeks of looking and aiming for joy. Research has shown that habits can be changed in eighteen to twenty-one days. Are you willing to give yourself three weeks to start walking on a path where you can meet your joy? I hope so. After twenty-one days, you may be changed. You may be so restored, so strengthened from looking for and finding joy that you may well be convinced that the pursuit of joy is worth your energy. I assure you that finding joy is possible, and will change your life. Joy is not hard to find, but it can be difficult to hold on to. Life sends us storms, and we forget we know sunshine. I say, remember the sunshine, and wait out the rain. Making notes about the good times can make joy easier to experience. Remembering a moment when you felt pure joy can bring that smile right back right away.

Take a few minutes to write down the joyous things that happen in your life. Practice this even if you see your joys as small. Just because something is small does not mean it does not exist.

For the next twenty-one days, commit to writing down at least one joyous moment you experience each day. If you experience two or three moments of joy, then list them each day. If your joys are large, grand, highly visible, write them down. But focus also on recording small joys. Use this time to train yourself not to let small joys escape your notice.

In our rushed and hectic lives, we need to slow down long enough to take notice of what makes us feel good, better, best. Are you reading this in springtime? Did you wake this morning to the sweet melody of robins singing outside your window? Are you reading this as autumn changes the color of the trees? Is your son or daughter enjoying school, learning well, growing up healthy? Do you hear your son's or daughter's or neighbor child's laughter? Do you have an elder in your midst? Have you heard words of wisdom from this elderly man or woman? Have you been in touch with old friends? Have you received an e-mail from an old college classmate? Has someone else offered you words of encouragement? Do you have a wife or husband or partner? Did you experience their warm embrace?

Notice the way the sunlight looks in your kitchen. Remember how you felt when you got your last phone call from a child away at school. Have you had a good blood pressure reading?

You get the idea.

Observing what brings you joy offers you more than just reflection, although reflection does have the great value of moving all of us toward a clearer examination of our lives. Knowing what brings us joy puts us in the important and beneficial position of being able to create more joy in our lives.

Maybe you will find that if you have your coffee at the kitchen table, you enjoy it more than when you take it to the car. A small change that would take you ten minutes to accomplish could bring on a better mood for the whole day. Or if you find that a good blood pressure reading brought you such a good feeling, stopping to make a note of this joyful feeling can strengthen your resolve and better your experiences. Seeing the reminder of what you've accomplished by lowering your blood pressure might help you manage your emotions and continue to be a little more careful about what you eat. You are more prone to reach the goal of another good reading if you have the experience of identifying and recording this joyful moment in your life.

Will you spend just a few minutes a day, for three weeks, testing, observing the moments when you feel joy? Working with your Joy Journal will show you how hope and faith engage optimism and joy. Write in your Joy Journal every day for twenty-one days and you will have a record of what inspires you, what makes you happy, what makes you pause. I believe you will smile more. Smiling is a sure sign of joy.

I have kept a Joy Journal at different times in my life. I have found that taking the time to make this record raised my awareness of simple pleasures and helped me keep my eye on the prize. I found that training my awareness on what lifted my spirits often helped me reach for bigger joys.

Keeping a Joy Journal helps you put yourself in the path of miracles. If you record the joys you experience, you become appreciative of what the universe and the Higher Power offer to you regularly. Like an athlete who must condition his or her body in order to win, you must condition your spirit in order to run your course through life.

Observing and recording your joys will help prime your spirit for positivity. Writing down what makes you joyful will help you "train your aim."

Train your aim? Absolutely. Everything we do—or do not do—in our lives is a function of what we choose, and what we intend. Even if we make a to-do list every day and accomplish *nothing* on that list, we have chosen, in whatever harried or hurried fashion, to let other issues take the place of what we wrote that we planned to do. Our lives require that we fashion our choices to meet not just our needs, but also our goals. We are responsible for carving out at least some little time to plant the seeds of what we ultimately want, and not just reap the harvest of what our lives have demanded that we do. For example, if we want to be well-read, then finding ten minutes a day to read a self-development book, a novel, or a news magazine is far better than not reading at all. Taking ten minutes a day toward a goal changes the day from a time of pure demand to a time of goal-getting, followed by a time of pure demand. I guarantee that if you pay attention to what brings you joy, your goal-getting will begin to incorporate those joys. When we continue to overlook what brings us joy, we run the risk of responding only to requirements and demands, and never drawing our goals any nearer to fulfillment.

Your Joy Journal will be a key tool in this transition from a demand-driven life to greater self-definition. Over time, your journal will become a short history of what brings you joy. In a matter of weeks, you will be able to look at your notes and use them to encourage you to do more to elevate your spirits and gladden your heart.

Do Yourself a Favor

Start and keep a Joy Journal as a favor to yourself for twenty-one days. You will be making a record, a road map of what you have to be thankful for and what you have to aim for. Think of it: you have already accomplished everything in your Joy Journal. Anything you do based on any note you write there will be a move forward, will be an advance. No one leads a joyless life, but without making a record of the joys we experience, we can loosely and casually behave as if there's little or nothing to celebrate.

A daily record of what brought you joy will help you stay on the positive path. Your listings do not necessarily need to be life-changing or earth-shattering—although sometimes they may be. But recording something good and positive that happened, that made this day better than its predecessor, is an important habit to develop. You can give yourself the gift of this habit in twenty-one days. This is an excellent exercise to help you notice what you are accomplishing, as well as see the stepping stones that you are already walking on.

Give yourself the grace of noting your good feelings, your daily accomplishments. Gratitude is an attitude. Keeping a Joy Journal is a fabulous technique to help you reach for and maintain the attitude you need.

A Joy Journal will also help clarify what you should be doing more of. Your Joy Journal will fuel your enthusiasm for life, and your enthusiasm will help keep your proverbial engine running.

You can list:	Or you can list:
Steps I took, or	Brilliant things my child said, or
Actions taken, or	Loving things my spouse said, or
Things I got done, or	Kind things my friend did, or
Problems I solved, or	The high point of the day, or
Bills I've paid, or	My first laugh today, or
Changes I've made.	My favorite song I heard today.

Do you get the point I'm making? Keep track of what makes a positive difference to you. Encourage yourself by recording your own daily actions, steps you've chosen to take that bring light to your life. Make sure that your well-deserved sleep does not erase the memory of the important work you are doing. Write your accomplishments down, jot down your joys.

Paying attention to the joy in your life is like opening window shades to sunshine. Keeping a Joy Journal will shine light on your accomplishments as you dare to make change. Paying attention to all you accomplish will inspire you to take the next step, and the next. This is how each one of us gets from point A to point B: by taking one step and then the next step and then the next. Let your Joy Journal help guide and inspire you.

Joy should not be taken for granted. Joy should not be overlooked. Joy is worth the ink and the time it takes to write a little note. The Joy Journal is worth the uplift that will result from your effort. Take twenty-one days, and see for yourself how much more positive you feel about the life you're living. Watch how noticing your joy will help you aim for more joy, and ultimately will motivate you to make your life better, more joyful, more closely related to the life you'd like to create.

If you are just beginning, or if this strategy is a leap for you, start gently. Hard as it is to imagine, seeking joy can be outside our comfort zone. Sometimes we are plain accustomed to distress and disarray. If someone asked you the question, "What gives you hope and what brings you joy?" would you be able to answer? Taking the time to work in a Joy Journal can inform you and give you insight. Taking the time to notice and reflect on what brings you joy will make you more competent at creating joy for yourself and sharing it with those you love.

Maybe you are not yet clear about what in your life brings you the most joy. Suppose you know that your children bring you joy, or that your hobbies bring you joy. Maybe you enjoy traveling or reading. Perhaps your accomplishments at work bring you joy. Have you ever considered joy itself, separately? Maybe you've not yet learned to pause and *experience* or *remember* joy as a current event. I believe that all of us have some experience with joy—though these events may be so small that we rush by them, pressed for time, barely noticing. This is why I cheerlead about the value of keeping a Joy Journal. In your own handwriting, in your own time, you can capture the joyful moment, real, even if small.

Maybe you have, like many of us, associated joy with the future: with times you dream of, with things you plan to do, with days to come. I encourage you to peer into your life for moments of joy now. Joy is like laughter or enthusiasm—it's infectious. I predict that taking the time to notice the joy in your life now will motivate you mightily to experience more joy. The joy you anticipate for your future might well come more quickly once you ride a joyful feeling for some of these first twenty-one days.

Your Joy Journal should be small in size—although it will have a big effect on you. You are only going to make short notes. No dissertations are necessary. The journal should be small enough to fit in a purse or a jacket pocket. You should be able to access your little book easily and quickly. If the book is too big to carry comfortably, or if you have to put it in your briefcase or your car, then you won't be able to write often enough.

If you were to jot down just a few joyful notes a day, even one a day, your small notebook will quickly fill. In order to really be able to keep a Joy Journal, you have to be prepared to be spontaneous. That's why your journal needs to be small enough to always carry, and easy to access quickly. You're making notes about what made you smile, made you grateful, brought you a good feeling. Having an opportunity to remember these things, to look back in your notebook and reflect on them at any time of day, can lift your spirit and can make a good day great.

Let me encourage you to change your program. Think joy. Reach for joy. Think about joy. Behave as if joy is your birthright. Write down small experiences of joy every day, and watch your joy multiply. Remember that the Joy Journal is just a list—a list of events, situations, or memories that you identify. Expect that this list is going to be a big help to you. Help yourself to joy.

Today:

Start your Joy Journal. Write down the one thing that gave you the most joy today. Identify for yourself why this brought you so much joy. Can you replicate this activity or experience time and time again?

Dare To...

Change your point of view.

- Begin looking for joyful options every day of your life.
- Understand what joy means to you; experience what joy feels like to you.

Adjust your behaviors.

- Actively create joyful moments as you spend the days of your life.
- Make a habit of seeking joy, and make notes of the joy you find.

Be resolute.

- Make your new habits hard to break.
- Insist that your life increase in joy, and take robust action to fulfill this requirement.

Four

Victim or Victorious?

We often overlook how many choices we have, because of the many real demands we face from day to day. We get into a routine. We have many people to attend to and to please. We rush, and we feel pressured to accomplish what our work demands, what our children require, and what our households need to keep running. And so often we don't or can't take the time to reflect on what choices we are actually making, and what choices we could make, if we would take the time.

When we wake up in the morning, even if we are exhausted, we have made the choice about what time we awake, about what time we set the alarm for. We make choices about what we feed our children, even if we buy the same foods at the grocery store week after week. We make choices about where we work, even if we've been at the same job for a very long time. Just because we are doing what we are required to do does not mean we have been stripped of choices. We always have a choice, if not about conditions, then at least about how we respond to our circumstances. In many instances, we even have choices about our circumstances. More often than not, we are in a place because we choose to be there.

Heroes Are Known for Struggle

Many of our heroes struggled through extreme circumstances. But they are heroes to us not just because of their circumstances, but also because of the choices they made in responding to those circumstances. Nelson Mandela used his time in prison to continue to reflect on and hope for the changed destiny of his country. In his book *Long Walk to Freedom*, he presents his efforts and mental discipline in great detail. Anne Frank, the persecuted teenager who faced *very* premature death, reflected on her condition with such care and discipline that her youthful writings continue to inspire and educate millions of children and adults. Both Mandela and Frank, whom we know as heroes, were constrained and imprisoned and yet found the determination to refuse to allow their minds or their thoughts to be crippled or silenced.

Nelson Mandela emerged from twenty-seven years in prison so strengthened that he was able to lead his country in its march to democracy. Anne Frank proclaimed that people really are good at heart even while she was literally being hunted. Her wisdom survives, although she was ultimately captured and killed by the Nazis *before her sixteenth birthday.*

We are inspired by those who, despite unbelievable pain and hardship, have chosen to become victors.

A combination of luck, tenacity, and faith permits some people to survive the most awful circumstances and rise again. For others, the slightest downturn turns them into victims for life. How is one ninety-year-old so beat down by aging body parts and diminished strength that he can barely make it through the day, while another is taking up new hobbies and traveling across the globe?

I am mystified by the idea that some of us fall into the deep hole of victimhood, yet others are able to soar, emerging victorious from our wrangles with life. Consider this fascinating and empowering truth: how we respond to even the worst of circumstances is, on many levels, a choice.

Victim or victorious? *What if the choice is really yours?*

I once had the honor to speak alongside Carla Harris, managing director in global markets at Morgan Stanley. Carla is a highly accomplished executive whose sensitivity to people is as sharp as her business acumen. The way she answered one person's question is something that I will never forget. It taught me and continues to inspire me years later.

The questioner, eager to learn Carla's formula for getting to the top of the corporate ladder, described her own situation and included a litany of constraints to her progress. She was born poor; she had earned an MBA from a "so-so" school; her MBA program did not offer the networking opportunities of other top schools; she was discriminated against because she was gay. She suffered from what appeared to be depression. She grew up in challenging circumstances, and so on. You get the idea.

Carla politely stopped the woman and said, "My sister, the very best advice I can give is that *you must decide to decide*—either you will be a victim or you will be victorious!"

Carla's clean, no-nonsense way of cutting to the heart of this very complex dynamic really got my attention. I could see by the look on the face of the questioner that she had been touched as well. My guess is that she, like so many others, never considered that she had a choice in the matter. In no way did Carla diminish this woman. But she presented the relatively revolutionary idea that although we may not have much say in what befalls us, *how we react and respond to our circumstances is totally within our power.*

Think about it—how many of us hold ourselves back because of past circumstances, poor decisions, or rotten luck? "My mother was domineering." "My family was dysfunctional." "I was sexually abused." "I drink to excess." "I lost my job." "I can't have children." "My husband left me with nothing but bills." "I'm discriminated against because of the color of my skin/my sexual preference/my religion/my gender."

Our lists of what we struggle through can be endless, especially if we remain focused on our difficulties. Concentrating on an issue, any issue, perpetuates and recreates what you are thinking of. If we spend our mental energy considering and reconsidering painful, hard-to-overcome circumstances, then we are basically working to keep those issues alive. In my courtroom, I hear litanies of problems every day. The obstacles we list, discuss, and complain about give us issues to hide behind. Too often we use our struggles as crutches. As long as we play the blame game, nobody will ever win. As long as we play the victim, we will never win.

Living a Nightmare

A young girl who came into my courtroom, Jamie, was first victimized by William, her mother's live-in boyfriend, when she was in sixth grade. For years thereafter, she was verbally and sexually abused—one of the most horrendous situations you can think of, the chronic abuse of a child. William threatened to kill Jamie's mother, Marie, if Jamie told anyone what was going on. After years of this horror, Jamie was no longer able to live with the shame and the agony. She confided in a trusted high school teacher. By then, Jamie was sixteen.

A warrant was issued for the arrest of her mother's live-in boyfriend, this despicable man. Jamie was promptly removed from the home by the state, taken to the hospital, and examined for signs of sexual abuse. She was placed in a temporary shelter pending an emergency hearing regarding her custody.

During her most vulnerable and formative years, Jamie had endured unimaginable, spirit-robbing abuse. In her child's mind, she endured these violations *in order to protect her mother.* Of course, once the truth was out in the open, Jamie imagined that her mother would come forth and protect her. She expected her mother to reach for her and comfort her. But sadly, that was not the case. Even in this state of crisis, Marie withheld the love and support her daughter so desperately needed.

Jamie's mom did not behave as most mothers would have. She did not rush immediately to the emergency room where her daughter had been taken to be examined. In the subsequent investigation, Marie repeatedly accused *Jamie* of improper behavior. Marie insisted that her boyfriend could never have done this. She said that Jamie was blaming this poor innocent man when in fact it was Jamie who had behaved improperly and was having sex as a young child! Not only had Marie failed to provide a safe haven for her daughter, but she also turned against her, siding with a disgusting sexual predator of a boyfriend. But Jamie had been up against these two dysfunctional adults her entire childhood—a man who had sexually abused her and a mother who had refused to protect her. Now their war was being waged in open court, and Jamie had taken steps to free herself from this brutality. Needless to say, the mother's lover was a no-show at the hearing. With his criminal behavior exposed, William fled, and was long gone by the court session. Marie answered police questions about him and, realizing she was on the verge of some pretty serious trouble, also disappeared, leaving Jamie standing alone.

To this day, I am still outraged by the fact that a mother chose this man, who by all evidence had not only sexually abused her daughter, but also held her as an emotional hostage with his threats to kill her mother. How dare she make this choice and simply disappear, leaving this child lingering in the foster care system? But that is what Jamie's unfit mother did, when she made a clear and despicable choice to cast her sorry lot with William, leaving her daughter to fend for herself.

Understandably, Jamie became despondent and confused: abused, lied to, accused of things she had never done; now, through no fault of her own, she was officially abandoned. Worse yet, she had protected her mother at her own peril. For years she had succumbed to abuse, suffering in silence and in fear that the cruel and vicious predator would kill her mother. But then when she needed her mother most, to protect and support her, Marie was nowhere to be found.

Jamie was placed in foster care. The prospects for adoption of this sixteen-year-old were poor. When she left my courtroom, I promised myself to stay in touch, and I did, chiefly through her wonderful social worker. I'm careful about making such promises, because it just isn't possible to follow the lives of so many people in need who pass through my courtroom. But I could see that maybe I could help this young girl, and I decided to try.

My instinct was correct. Although parentless and in foster care (not the best environment for building self-esteem and resilience), Jamie began to grow emotionally stronger. She devoted herself to her studies and was eventually able to focus on a dream—to one day attend a prestigious college and earn a degree in social work.

Talk about transformation! This young woman was able to give voice to the horror that had befallen her and use it for good. She wrote about her past and her dreams for the future in an essay contest that won her a scholarship.

When I learned that she would attend college, I told Jamie I would do everything in my power to be there when she graduated. Those of you familiar with me know that watching "my kids" graduate is one of my biggest joys. I work very hard to attend graduations, especially for those children who have to really work against victimhood in order to accomplish the major goal of finishing school. In fact, it's become a custom for me to celebrate each of these successes by showing up "with bells on." My refrain is this: I'll be there to see you with a new dress, a new hat, and a new pair of shoes! This has been my customary signal that their achievement means a great deal to me. I want each of my "Jamies" and "Jeramies" to see me in the front row and to know just how much I honor their tenacity and achievement.

I was ultimately disappointed to learn that the day of Jamie's graduation would conflict with another obligation. I had previously agreed to be a commencement speaker at another school. But we worked it out—I attended Jamie's baccalaureate service the day before, and then I flew out to the other graduation.

I was honored to sit in the front row as Jamie proudly marched in with her classmates. We hugged and it just felt wonderful. I've attended many of these events over the years and it's hard to describe the joy. Jamie's ceremony was no exception.

There she sat, lovely and composed, looking no different for her incredible trials than the students who surrounded her, students who had had the blessings of family support at every turn. Yet Jamie had nurtured, *for herself*, a very different person, wiser, more battered, and more determined than most twenty-two-year-olds.

Choose Victory

When you're feeling victimized by loss or disappointment and unable to take that first step out of the darkness, I hope you'll think about this amazing young woman. I wonder if my retelling even does her story justice. To see a young girl, so completely victimized and unsupported, gather her strength and make her way forward is a sign that every one of us can shift out of victim status and pursue what would be victory for each of us in our individual lives.

That each of us has our own unique blueprint to victory is a blessing. Like Jamie, we all can begin *from where we are.*

Jamie's actions and her example strengthen and inspire me to this day. I think about her, and others like her, sometimes when I need to gather my strength and go on.

By the way, this remarkable young lady *has* fulfilled her dream. She is now employed as a social worker working with abused children. Jamie has demonstrated her victory over her past. She has dedicated her life's work to alleviating the suffering of children, something she knows all too well. Isn't it absolutely fitting that children are benefiting from her invaluable perspective?

Jamie chose victory over victimhood. Every victory, for anyone, results from the pursuit of our goals. Without actually seeking victory, without taking specific action to achieve our visions or dreams, no success is possible. Jamie dared to dream, and then she pursued that dream despite devastating odds and a very bad start. Jamie moved from a place of misery to a place of promise. You can be assured that she was constantly telling herself that she could accomplish the goals she set for herself. Jamie convinced herself that she could pass through the tragic times and meet herself where she dreamed of being—safe, changed, strong. In order to achieve victory, in order to accomplish her goals, I'm sure her self-talk was about what she could make happen, not about the tragedies that had already happened. We have to train our minds to see ourselves gaining victory. Where our minds lead, our energies follow.

When I think of Jamie, I can't help but contrast her story with the many purposeless youngsters who appear in my courtroom. I don't refer just to the "have-nots." I've also seen a lot of overprivileged young lawbreakers who had money in their pockets and drove to school in a nice little BMW. Spoiled rotten and selfish to the core. These young people need to change their self-talk as well. This is the critical and fundamental and *transformational* truth about victory: all success is, at least at first, self-defined. None of us can achieve what we cannot see or envision for ourselves. No amount of luck will change a visionless life to a victorious life. This is why so many winners of big lottery prizes lose all they've won, and sometimes end up worse off than before. In order to be successful, rich, influential, or in any way victorious, each of us *must* be able to see ourselves as successful, rich, influential, or victorious *first*.

Jamie managed to do what she needed to. She managed to convince her number one asset—herself—that she was pursuing a goal she could attain. How many thousands of times must she have had to remind herself? Maybe millions of times. Thoughts move fast, and have far-reaching effects. Her self-talk must have centered around inspiration—telling herself that she was capable, that she was worthy, that she had escaped her long-term disaster. Jamie propelled herself into a space of opportunity, and in order to overcome "what used to be true," I'm certain that she had to talk herself through to victory.

Take the challenge. Talk yourself through to victory. Decide what victory would mean, *for you*. Envision yourself achieving what you would accomplish if you were able. Remember that you *are* able. Remember that seeing yourself successful is the *first* step. After you take consistent and determined action, you will move yourself from where you are toward the vision that you have. Continue to cultivate your vision. Remember Jamie: in six years, she went from being an abused child to becoming a college graduate. Hold on to your vision. Give yourself two years, or six years, or longer. Acknowledge that achieving your dream is worthy of your attention, even if you work toward it for decades.

If you do not work toward your dream, the years will still pass by. If you do envision yourself victorious and work toward that image of your victory, then as the years pass by you will be accomplishing your goals.

Are you holding on to a situation where you feel you have been victimized and you are not able to move beyond it? Were you abused as a child? Does that abuse keep you from living your fullest life? I strongly recommend that you seek counseling now. Perhaps you are the victim of domestic violence. You deserve to live a life free of violence and chaos. If counseling is not effective for your partner, or if your abusing partner is unwilling, immediately make a plan to extract yourself from that situation. Your life could depend on it.

Maybe you are a victim in a different way. Perhaps you are being disrespected in an intimate relationship or undervalued in your job, or a trusted confidant betrayed your privacy and has tried to ruin your reputation.

Maybe you have made yourself a victim, telling yourself that you are not worthy to be happy or successful or prosperous ...

Life is too precious for you to continue to live as a victim. Devote yourself to your purpose, and live life victoriously.

Today:

Honestly ask yourself, are you choosing victory in your life? If not, what one thing do you need to begin working on today to become victorious? Think carefully about the victory you seek: stop and anticipate the joy you will feel when you are victorious. Write down the one step you want to take, and then execute what you have written, with joyful anticipation in mind.

Dare To...

Move beyond defeats, however devastating.

- Think of heroes like Nelson Mandela or Anne Frank. Know that heroes are not remembered for defeat.
- Accept that you are *the* hero in your own life.

Get up, even though you have fallen down.

- Accept that every person falls down in their life.
- Learn your lessons and go on.

Stay devoted to your vision, even if change is decades in coming.

- Welcome your goals when they arrive.
- Expect success, and never stop working toward it—day by day.

Five

Find Purpose and Passion in All That You Do

Many of us work hard, or work for years, or both, without feeling any love for the work we do. We trade the time of our lives for a paycheck—and certainly, all of us need our paychecks—but too often we are living like a paycheck is worth living for.

Of course, as a matter of principle, we know better. We would all admit the truth that life should be more than a paycheck—even as our quest for pay dominates our lives. Some of us wonder how to find more in life, beyond our jobs and our salary. Our hearts tell us that there's more. Many of us feel incomplete or unfulfilled. But we find it hard to identify what we're missing.

Passion is what we're missing. Understanding, honoring, and acknowledging what drives and motivates us is absolutely key to living

a satisfying life. Many of us ignore our passions. We sacrifice and separate from what we are really motivated to do, as we settle into doing the
work we can find to support ourselves and our families in the best way
possible. Many of us have not been able or have not made the effort to
fill our lives—even the earning part of our lives—with work that we feel
strongly about.

Choosing work to sustain ourselves is an honorable choice, but as
complex human beings living in a complex society, our needs are not
that simple. All of us have higher needs—to be fully occupied, to devote
our time to fulfilling tasks, to feel like we are making a difference. Our
passions will generally point us in these directions, if we dare to pay
attention to what we are truly motivated to do. For those of us who
have spent years ignoring our true interests, a part of us that we have
ignored begins to ache for our energy and attention too.

When we are required to overcome tough times in our lives, doing
what we are motivated to do can revive us, can energize us. When we
are engaged in life with vigor and energy, we are stronger and more
able to weather life's difficulties.

Once we get in touch with our passion, or at least learn its name,
our lives are often transformed, and our degree of attachment to our
lives is shifted. Tuning into what really motivates us leads us to opportunities that will fulfill us in multiple ways. Finding a way to shape our
lives around our own energy and motivation can mean the difference
between surviving and thriving.

We all have trials—barely sufficient income, the needs of growing children, the worry of aging parents, a glass ceiling, unpromising work,
emergencies, divorces, layoffs. Yet any of us who has ever struggled
knows that the difference between just living and living well is huge.
In order to exit crisis mode, the bridge between surviving and thriving

is absolutely critical to cross. We owe it to ourselves and to our spirits to cross over from the stressful shores onto the riverbank of rewarding lives. Passion marks the way to the bridge.

Doing work or being committed to something that we *really* care about helps us get out of our own way. Finding a way to make our work matter to us and to others allows us to move beyond today's problems. I know some people seem to have been born with their passion already in place. All they seem to have to do is pursue it. Some people know what they require, and do not flounder through life making choices that violate their heart's desires. Some people, it seems, are born with a passion for painting or business, music or leadership. Others know from childhood that teaching disabled students, for example, is where they will find satisfaction. But for most of us the search is less direct.

Passion Solves Problems

You've no doubt heard amazing stories about how someone's life was transformed by discovering and attending to his or her passions. In fact, I argue that the most amazing shifts in people's lives have passion as an ingredient. What about you? Do you know what stirs your soul? Have you followed your instincts—even when others recommended otherwise? Have you discovered the work, hobby, activity, or cause that brings you peace, satisfaction, calm, or joy?

Passion is different from skill. It's really important to discover the difference between these two. Consider a student who was great at math. She consistently excelled and decided to see where her skill could take her professionally. Computer programming was a logical next step and she took it. Only problem is, she hated the field. Her heart wasn't in it and the work became a painful grind.

After years of feeling dull and disengaged at work, she decided to pursue a master's degree in teaching, following a strong hunch that her passions might surface in the classroom. She was right, and adores teaching middle school math. Now that she's successfully combined her skill with her passion, she has found both peace and purpose.

Now when she pulls out her papers and lesson plans for the day, she also unloads passion and excitement. Her workdays are energizing. She feels open to life and is able to give back a great deal to her students.

I became a lawyer early in my life, and I have always enjoyed the work. I especially liked my nine-year stint in the legal department of Delta Air Lines, where I imagined I would spend my entire career. As fate and faith would have it, that did not happen. I left Delta, and was sworn in as Chief Presiding Judge of the Fulton County Juvenile Court. Becoming a judge was a heady and humbling time. At the swearing in, my parents stood to my left and my children stood to my right, holding the Bible on which I promised to uphold the law. Looking back, I see now that at that moment my path was redefined. I followed my interests, and I was about to discover my passion.

Although difficult and heartrending, the cases that flooded my calendar my first week were typical of what would come. There were children stuck in foster care for years without a permanent home, a fifteen-year-old armed robber, and a baby whose parents were simply too sick to care for him anymore.

The first child on my calendar that morning happened to be an adorable eight-year-old who was ushered in by his social worker, Beth. This precious little boy stood silently, gazing around the courtroom as if expecting to see something or someone familiar. Eventually, he began to tremble, as if his whole soul was being drained from him. I could see him from the bench as he began to shake. It rattled my heart.

Seeming so very frightened, he was an alarming sight to watch. Instinctively I stood up, unzipped my black robe, and started to climb down from the bench to take him into my arms.

"Hold on, Judge! You can't come down here," the bailiff called out. I don't know what he thought would befall me or what I was coming down to do, but clearly my action was not proper procedure, at least not from the bailiff's perspective.

"You'd better get out of my way. This is my courtroom!" I retorted. The truth is, I had been a mama a whole lot longer than I had been a judge. What was I propelled by? Perhaps maternal instinct, or sadness, or a desire to change this boy's sad circumstances. I did not stop to assess exactly what propelled me—I just continued down the steps, knelt, and took this frightened little boy in my arms and held him. He never cried. He continued to tremble, though, soundlessly, so small and so sad.

I didn't know then what I know now. This little boy was one of my first cases, and over time he became a symbol to me of children in distress. I have seen countless children like him in my courtrooms by now. Children of different ages—some small, some half grown, some near grown. All the neglected children arrive in court because we have failed them in some way. Their stories differ. Some of them are brought in or accompanied by a grandmother or other relative. More often than anyone would think, the children come to court with perfect strangers. Yet they all have been failed by somebody. The common theme is that someone didn't keep a promise to them, and that's why they ended up in court with me.

Someone promised to come back and never returned. Someone promised to take care of them and instead ran off with the drug man. Someone promised to be a parent and was not. Someone promised to love and protect them and instead abused and neglected them. So many kids end up with me because of so many broken promises. The problem is that for children especially, broken promises create broken lives.

When this wondering, small child peered around the courtroom, he wasn't just glancing idly. He was looking for his mother, Lynn. His mother had been subpoenaed, but was nowhere to be found. That day in court, there was nobody familiar and nothing this little boy knew.

In late July, the little boy's mother had left him at a shelter where the two had been staying. She told him she would be back, and she never returned. The authorities at the shelter contacted the Georgia Division of Family and Children Services (DFACS).

Of course, DFACS had to take the little boy into their custody. They placed him in a temporary shelter/safe house for children at risk. For *ten weeks*, she did not return. I have spent my share of time observing these places, and they are as sad as you dare to imagine. Children are abruptly disrupted, removed from their regular circumstances, and sent to a strange place filled with other children, many of whom spend their first days and nights literally wailing with sorrow and loss.

When this child's mother did not come back to the shelter as promised and he was forced into the children's shelter, he believed with all his heart that if he could just hold on until he came to court, surely his mother would be there. Some other child, perhaps, must have mentioned to him that when you go to court, you see your mother again. For months, he bravely clung to the hope that his mother would appear when he arrived in court and take him with her.

The purpose of the October hearing was to come up with a plan and a set of expectations for Lynn to ensure the little boy's welfare. But Lynn failed to appear in court. It is easy to imagine that empty is exactly how this young boy must have felt, day after day, waiting for a mother he could not believe would just walk out on him. With no other family and an unknown father, the little boy was for all intents and purposes abandoned. At eight, a child knows that "I'll be back to get you" means this afternoon, not later this year. I could only imagine that his wait seemed endless. His wait *was* endless. And worse yet, unfulfilled.

I still cannot imagine being eight years old and not having anyone in the world to hold on to. Not a mother, not a father, not a grandmother, a brother, cousin, aunt, uncle—not anyone. He had every reason to stand there that morning trembling in my courtroom.

All of the little boy's hopes focused intently on this one morning, this particular hour in my courtroom. He trembled from despair and disappointment. Watching him was nearly more than I could manage.

Like this worried, anxious child, I had no idea what the future would bring. But what I did know was that, then and there, my passion found me. I pulled back from embracing him so I could look this precious little boy in the eye and said to him, "Listen, I know you're looking for your mother. I am not going to lie to you. I don't know where she is. But I will promise you that I am going to do everything in my power to find her. Do you think you can hold on just a little bit longer?"

The little boy said nothing, just looked at me. I was a stranger who had reached out to him, kneeling on the floor. What could he have been thinking? Whether he could put faith in my promise was anybody's guess. All he knew for sure was that his mother, his touchstone and his key to the world, remained missing and had not come back for him.

I left this worried little boy in the care of his case worker and walked back up the steps to the bench. As I zipped up my robe, I made a decision that might have seemed ridiculous to the people in the closed hearing, but to me it was clearly what urgently needed to be done. Whether we could find her or not, we at the very least had to try.

"I'm recessing this case and am issuing a warrant for the arrest of Lynn Johnson for failure to appear in court," I announced. "We will reconvene at two p.m. Not thirty days from now, not next week, but two p.m. *this afternoon.*"

The bailiff protested, "But, but . . ."

"But nothing," I responded. "With all the deputy sheriffs in this county we ought to be able to find this mother. At the very least we ought to try! It's up to this court to move urgently and aggressively on behalf of this child. He's lingered too long."

The disbelief in the courtroom was almost audible. I had proposed something that either reflected my lack of experience or confirmed for most that the new judge was absolutely out of her mind. Such searches can take weeks, if not months. I had allowed five hours for the sheriff's department to locate a woman who had been missing for more than two months. If climbing off the bench to take this little boy in my arms was unusual, expecting that the mother could be found in half a day was equally unprecedented. (As I hope you'll learn in your own experience, finding and following passion can lead you down some uncharted pathways!)

The illogical nature of my action did not escape me. But I was consumed with the image of this child, pathetically alone in the center of the courtroom, abandoned, disappointed, and so unsure of the future.

The Endless Wait

At 1:30 p.m., a proud deputy walked up the courthouse steps with Lynn Johnson in custody. When I was notified that she had been found, I said to the sheriff, "Please get her some coffee—let's make sure she's good and sober." (At the time I had no idea that coffee would have no effect on a crack high. Having seen what I've seen since, it seems laughable now that I ever would have imagined such an easy solution. Live and learn!)

By 2 p.m., we resumed. Beth, the case worker, had taken the little boy back to the shelter. But standing before me was a woman who was belligerent, fidgety, unable to focus, out of control, and wholly lacking in remorse. Unable to identify herself as the source of her child's pain, she was surly with me, and angry at her defenseless child. She acted as if the whole thing was a huge inconvenience.

It was all I could do not to go off on this woman. My rational side reminded me that I had just taken the judicial oath one week ago and I needed to keep my temper in check. My other, emotional side violently disagreed. How could I not react from the heart to a woman who had caused so much pain to her child?

The two sides reconciled and I told myself, *You may feel justified, but don't go off on this woman, Glenda. It's not going to resolve the matter.* I took a couple of deep breaths and calmed down. I planned to proceed straight by the book.

"Ms. Johnson," I said, with a reserve I did not feel. "I'd like to ask you a few questions. The first is, why did you abandon this child while you went and got high in a lousy crack house?"

Lynn played the fool, shrugging her shoulders.

I was trying with all my heart to remain calm, but my voice was rising. "How dare you abandon your child for two and a half months and come here with no remorse and no accountability?"

Sober or not, this woman turned out to be absolutely out of control. When she replied to my questions, nothing she said made any sense; clearly we were dealing with a loose cannon, and a badly addicted parent. I hesitated a minute while I silently asked God for the strength to do right by this little boy who was now depending on me to help.

"Ma'am," I started back in, "I do not play when it comes to children. Now, I'm asking you in a court of law whether you're ready to do what you need to do to get your son back."

I turned to Beth and asked that she develop a case plan that would include a thirty-day inpatient drug treatment and a review hearing in forty-five days. I had envisioned that this little boy could be home with his mother for Christmas. I ordered her to treatment and a future hearing and banged my gavel to signal my resolve. What I would learn was that it would take so much more, especially when the woman I was ordering was a serious crack addict who had no remorse about abandoning her child.

Forty-five days later we met back in the courtroom and it was clear that Lynn Johnson had not complied with my order. She hadn't been near a drug treatment center and, worse yet, had made no effort to contact her son. Again, I was faced with a woman who was belligerent and out of control. I turned to the court reporter and directed that we go off the record. There were things I wanted to say that I didn't think the court of appeals would necessarily understand! Mercifully, the reporter's clacking keys fell silent.

"Ms. Johnson," I began, "you now have two choices: either you get your life together and decide to become the kind of parent your child deserves, or I will step down from the case and assign it to another judge, which will legally permit me to strongly recommend that DFACS aggressively move to terminate your parental rights and make him available for adoption to a family that will love and nurture him. He deserves to be in a home, not a shelter. I am not going to let him grow up in foster care!"

Her blasé demeanor turned to anger and defiance at the suggestion of adoption.

"No way, Judge, nobody would adopt him because he's too old to be adopted!" Lynn offered blithely. Now not only was she abdicating her parenting duties, she was trying to tell me that nobody else would want her child.

Totally disgusted, I leaned over the bench and said, "I will come down off this bench and kick your ass."

As I had told her the first time she appeared before me, I do not play when it comes to children. By this point I had abandoned any concern about exceeding proper boundaries. I was acting out of pure . . . passion. In retrospect, I can't actually believe I said this, but I realized that it truly turned the tide. How dare she be so cavalier about her child's life?

My boiling rage reduced to a simmer and I sat back down in my "judge chair" and looked at Lynn. I felt as if I were in slow motion—a kind of passionate calm had come over me as I continued. I believe it was at that moment that I truly got her attention. I addressed her in a more nurturing voice.

"Lynn, I am a mother too. I have two sons who mean absolutely the world to me. There is no way I would *ever, ever* let a stranger come into my home in the middle of the night and take my children. I'm not a violent person, but I would fight with everything in me to prevent that. In fact, I'm quite certain I would give up my own life to save theirs. Does that make sense to you?"

She nodded her agreement, unsure, as I was, where this was all leading. But fortunately the right words came forth, words I now know were fueled by passion. "Lynn, I want you to try to picture your drug addiction as a dangerous stranger who's broken into your home in the middle of the night and is trying to drag this little boy out the door with him." This literally poured out of me—straight from my heart to my mouth with no judicial filter.

"Lynn, you have got to *fight* your addiction with every ounce of your being, just like you'd fight that intruder. You have to look at your drug addiction like a stranger coming in and robbing you of the greatest gift in your life—your son."

At that moment, she looked at me with a flicker of understanding. Our eyes locked for a moment—an all-important moment—and only then did I feel I had reached her. She admitted, in court, that she was an addict and that she needed and wanted help. This time, she agreed to go into treatment and to follow the case worker's plan. With tears in her eyes, she said she very much wanted her little boy back. I came off the bench to give her a hug of encouragement. I did not promise her that it would be easy. I just promised her that the steps she was taking were necessary, because she was fighting for her life and she was fighting for her son. I promised her that it would all be worth it—not easy, but so worth it.

The courtroom cleared, and I had a minute to reflect on what had happened. I realized that I was feeling okay about all this. I may have gone about it unconventionally, but we had managed to get this woman on an important new path. And we were beginning to envision where it all might end up, provided Lynn could make good on her promises.

I realized I was feeling something new—a feeling I had never experienced at any other "job." Without question I had come to a place of passion, a place from which I never wanted to retreat.

For the next few months I monitored Lynn's progress and there were significant ups and downs. She exhibited the sort of zigzag pattern that can accompany lasting change. Sadly, the sweet little boy did not make it home for Christmas that year, as I hoped he would. Despite

Lynn's efforts she relapsed at least twice. But ultimately she did complete her drug treatment program.

She was working on being clean and sober and was regularly attending meetings of AA and NA (Narcotics Anonymous). The little boy and Lynn had been having successful supervised visitations, trying to rebuild the trust that had been so badly broken. The process took considerably longer than I had thought.

Late afternoon on Christmas Eve of the following year I was in the office tending to some end-of-the-year orders and other paperwork. Most of the staff had left for Christmas break and the court offices were cloaked in that kind of pre-holiday emptiness that feels so different from a regular Friday.

Out of the silence, my phone rang. It was Beth. "Judge, I am so happy I found you in! We can get Lynn's little boy back home today, but I need you to sign this order before I can do anything." I told her I would be so pleased to sign the order. I knew that the social worker was very close to recommending that custody be returned to Lynn and was thrilled at the prospect that he would get to go home in time for Christmas. Lynn had worked hard to see this day.

By about 4 p.m. we had finished the paperwork and Beth was on her way to get the little boy and escort him back home. I thanked her for her incredible work on the case. She said to me, "Judge, I know it meant so much to you to have him back home by Christmas and I did everything I could to make it happen." We both had tears in our eyes; we hugged each other tightly, acknowledging the long path to this moment.

Getting that precious little boy back where he belonged took a huge effort on the part of everyone involved, beginning with the little boy himself—who had faith and desire enough for all of us. His mother,

Lynn, his social worker, Beth, and I, a judge who had found her passion, all had to band together to help raise this child up from dislocation and despair. I pushed and worked and threatened and cajoled. I did everything I could—because in trying to restore balance in this child's life, I found my passion, and my passion found me.

Passion Keeps You Going

A week into my new job as juvenile court judge I knew that I had been called away from a cushy and enjoyable position at Delta Air Lines for a reason. I knew there would be many painful moments ahead—incredibly sad cases that might even test my faith. Cases that would certainly cause me to catch my breath, and pray for strength. But after working this little boy's case, I knew for sure that I was where I was supposed to be. I felt burning passion about the work I was doing.

I put my stake in the ground that October many years ago. My attention and intention remain with this work more securely now than ever. I have moved from the Fulton County Juvenile Court to a TV courtroom, but my commitment to children and families has not wavered, and has only increased. The fire in my belly I felt when I first knelt down by that abandoned eight-year-old boy is as true to me today as it was way back when.

Passion keeps you going. Passion keeps you strong.

I believe God was acting through me when he put me in the path of children and their challenges. Not just the innocent victims like that little boy but fifteen-year-old paid assassins, thirteen-year-old prostitutes, and gang members who murder without remorse.

I've prayed dozens of times, "Lord, give me the strength to not be paralyzed by these tragedies. Help me shift my energy from grieving to action. Help me help the children you've put before my hands."

There is no guarantee that finding our passion will make anything easy. But finding our passion will make life make more sense.

I am often asked, how do I find my passion? You now know from reading my story that my passion and my purpose intersected that morning in that courtroom. My advice is simple but not necessarily easy to implement. You must be in tune with your heart's desires, and you must listen carefully to your inner voice.

I had a dear friend and colleague, Stacey Sauls, leave the law department of Delta and attend seminary to become an Episcopalian priest. My first reaction was, *What the hell are you doing?* mainly because he was a phenomenal lawyer and an even better friend. Selfishly, I did not want him to leave. As successful as he was as a lawyer, his soul yearned to be of service to people and to tend to their spiritual needs. I so love and respect him for following his heart and aligning his purpose and passion. He dared to take charge of his life.

What is it that you love, that you would be happiest doing? Is it teaching, is it composing music, is it being a social worker helping people in need? Is it being a stay-at-home parent nurturing your children, or is it negotiating a contract for your firm?

Your passion may be found outside what you do professionally. Are you most engaged and fully alive when you are preparing for a marathon, volunteering at a food bank, or campaigning for a political candidate? Let there be something in your life that you are passionate about and then be intent on living your life on purpose.

Today:

Write down the three things you are most passionate about in your life. How are these passions manifested in your life currently? How would you like to see these passions manifested in your life in the future?

Dare To...

Find your passion and let your passion fuel your life.

- Understand that your passion in life is closely related to what you describe as intuition—which feels like God.
- Know that your passion relates closely to your purpose.

Be intentional about your purpose in life.

- You can know your passion without taking any action. But when you intentionally incorporate your passion into your actions and decision-making, you permit yourself to become more whole.
- Experience the real strength and energy that passion can create as you make choices that support you and support your heartfelt purpose.

Expect to get stronger.

- Define, acknowledge, and act on your passion, which will bring you much closer to who you really are, and who you hope to become.
- Be *directed* on the journey of life. Look to your passion to help you chart your course and to strengthen your resolve that you have chosen correctly.

Six

Do the Best You Can with What You've Got

Doing the very best we can with what we have on hand is a kind of mantra that some of us have become immune to, I think. Sometimes, when our ideas are deeply internal, or when we say things over and over, we believe we mean them, and we do, but at the same time, we've stopped actually hearing the real meaning of what we're saying.

I'm reminded of people who I hear saying, "Love you." And the words ring in the wind. "Love you, too," is the same. Or, for myself, when I try to say, "Thank you," expressing my gratitude to the many people in my life who offer help or support, I always *mean* "thank you" when I say those words, but I find that in order to make an impression on the person, about my real need to express gratitude, I often have to repeat myself. "Thank you, thank you, thank you," I hear myself saying. I can only hope that the person I'm talking to *really* hears me.

The idea of *doing the very best you can* has met a similar fate over time. Hopefully we start hearing this directive when we are children. We tell our children that we're less concerned with competition and that we are most concerned with their *doing their best.* By the time we are teenagers and adults, we try to calm ourselves by requiring "just our best," however things turn out. But maybe you realize, as I do, that as adults we are often *soothing* ourselves for something that hasn't worked as we've planned, when we say, "Well, I did my best." Or when we are about to perform a task and we don't expect that we'll have all the success we might want, we say to ourselves, again in resignation, "I can only do my best."

Wake Up "Your Best"

I'm here to wake up the notion of "your best." I ask you to think of not just your best, but your *very best.* Here's the real truth: when we do our very best, we often exceed expectations. We surpass what we thought we could do, and we vault over what others are expecting as well. When we do our very best with individual tasks we set out to complete, we are able to give a special level of attention to what we're doing. Our *very* best actually starts and ends with our attention to what we are trying to do. Our actions actually follow our thoughts. So when we begin a project, however small, and do our *very best*, that means that we first bring our full attention and our best thoughts to what we are endeavoring to accomplish. After we think through what we're trying to accomplish, using our full attention, then we take the steps that our mental planning process has generated. By thinking first, then planning, and by doing both of these with our full attention on the task, we can move into action with a head start.

Doing our very best does not mean we start by doing. Our minds are one of our primary divine gifts. Doing our very best requires that we devote the best mental energy we have to every task we say is important to us. Only after we have engaged our thinking do we take action—when we are doing our very best. When we take action and complete the action we have intended to take, most of the time the work is not done. One action hardly ever completes a task; one action only rarely allows us to accomplish our goal.

Accept this challenge. Renew your acquaintance with your very best. Take just today, or even take just the next hour. Think about what you are doing, think about what you are going to do next. Get clear, in your mind, about what doing *your very best* means for each action. If doing your very best means leaving for work ten minutes earlier so you don't have to rush or risk being late, then offer yourself that peace, give yourself less stress this morning, and leave ten minutes earlier. If doing your very best means accepting that you often don't do your very best, then accept it, and consider this an opportunity to discover what can happen for you if you begin to do your very best, today.

The Snowball Effect

Start small. It doesn't take long for this effort to snowball. Once you start asking your mind and spirit to join you in doing your very best, you will begin to feel so empowered. You will become miraculously aware of how much power you have within you. You will *feel* great control. You are in charge of whether and when you do your very best. But once you do your very best, you will be happily in charge of what you do, how much you do, and how well you do. I predict you will feel eagerness—to do your very best at the smallest tasks, to apply your mental energy to tasks you haven't given much thought to, to take on new challenges and see how much you can accomplish.

Reviving your experience with your very best is going to reap huge results. As I've said, there are many actions involved in even the most straightforward tasks. I want you to try to do your very best *with each action*. This will be how you create "the snowball effect."

The Warrick Dunn Story

Warrick Dunn, who some of you may know from the Atlanta Falcons, is one of the most purposeful and focused people I know. Once named the league's Offensive Rookie of the Year, Warrick has had a long and distinguished career with the NFL and has earned multiple Pro Bowl selections. As a member of the Falcons's board, I was honored to get to know Warrick during his years in Atlanta.

Warrick's character soars both on and off the field. In preparing to write this chapter, I talked with him to learn more about the path that led him to such incredible success.

Warrick played quarterback, cornerback, and running back in high school in Louisiana. He helped lead Catholic High in Baton Rouge to the state championships, for the first time ever. In January of his senior year in high school, Warrick's mother, Betty Smothers, was ambushed and killed by robbers. She worked in a store as an off-duty police officer to supplement her regular income. Betty Smothers was a loving and dedicated single mother who headed a household that included Warrick and five younger children.

Warrick lost his mother two days after his eighteenth birthday, a time of life when many young men, certainly many high school football stars, are concerned about little beyond the immediate excitement of high school and the prospects of college. The opposite proved to be true for young Warrick Dunn. Practically overnight, Warrick turned his attention to becoming an ultra-responsible adult. This was a choice he made, and those of us who know him admire his maturity and determination.

Following his mother's death, Warrick decided that he would keep his siblings together under one roof, and that he would raise them. "Lots of times I think about that night my mom was shot and killed," Warrick said. "I sometimes wonder why she raised me the way she did. She always trusted me to help make decisions for the family, training me to be a man when I was still a boy. I believe she was preparing me for the time when I would have to be that guy—the man of the house."

The easier solution would have been to send the kids to relatives. Lots of members of his family pressured him to do just that, except for his grandmother, who supported his decision to keep the family intact. Warrick really had to rely on everybody in that family to pull together. Teamwork was his model. Accustomed to executing plays decisively, he knew that by taking action, by reconsidering after each play, and by taking new actions toward his goal, he could set his plan in motion and work to keep his family together. Warrick's big picture was the total of what he wanted to achieve, but he understood that there would be *many steps* involved. Warrick focused on doing his very best, with each task, one action at a time.

Warrick moved forward through the pain of losing his beloved mom. Warrick's mother had sacrificed mightily for her children, and clearly had great confidence in her eldest son. She left an insurance policy in Warrick's name. Warrick considered his options; he brought his *thinking* to the table. He maturely and intelligently chose to use the proceeds from the policy to purchase a new home. He moved the family out of the rented house in which they'd been living.

"Honestly, I could have been selfish and done my own thing with the money, but I really tried to follow my heart and do the things Mama would have wanted me to do. I got advice from people I respected, and used it to help me make my decisions. And I got input from everyone in the family. I decided we would use the money to get a house and that nothing was going to separate us. Not the city, not the state, nobody."

Warrick's maternal grandmother moved in with her grandchildren, a true blessing. This helped Warrick especially, as he was wrestling with difficult decisions about college. Although he had made plans before his mother's death to attend Florida State, he was now forced to reconsider. Staying close and playing for Louisiana State University was a possibility that would let him keep a closer eye on his brothers and sisters. But his grandmother assured him that she could handle things on the home front, so he headed to Florida.

Although Warrick enjoyed school, he never became completely comfortable with the campus scene. He gave his attention to the classroom and the football field; he was too preoccupied for a typical social life and college fun. Warrick returned home to Baton Rouge every chance he got, to see for himself that his brothers and sisters were on the right path—doing their homework, bringing home good grades, and behaving for their grandmother. He devoted his vacations to his brothers and sisters. "I never spent the summers in Tallahassee. I'd always come home and focus on the family," he says.

Warrick graduated from Florida State with a degree in Information Studies. He left behind an impressive string of rushing records and was a three-time all-ACC selection. Not surprisingly, he was selected in the first round NFL draft by the Tampa Bay Buccaneers. He quickly proved his value to the Bucs organization and was named to the Pro Bowl team.

But Warrick did not arrive in Tampa alone. His three youngest siblings moved with him to Florida to attend high school. To say the least, a twenty-two-year-old head of household and three teenagers was not your typical NFL family. "I tried to be father and brother at the same time," says Warrick. "I made sure they did their homework, I attended parent-teacher conferences, I cooked, and I went to all their games."

In a wise parenting strategy many twice his age haven't figured out, Warrick dedicated one night a week as family night. The Dunns would go out to dinner and sit and talk together, catching up and staying close.

Nights on the road were not easy. Warrick experienced the typical pull familiar to so many parents whose work takes them out of town. "I'd never go out with the team. I'd head right back to the hotel and get on the phone with the kids." Warrick's focus was exemplary—he was all about family and football, with very few distractions. The party life common within the league was just not something he made time for.

The year after he joined the Bucs, Warrick Dunn did permit himself one significant and worthwhile "distraction." He created Homes for the Holidays, a nonprofit organization established in memory of his dear mother and that honors her dream of homeownership. Through this organization, Warrick acknowledged the importance of the home in keeping his own siblings strong and connected.

Homes for the Holidays was introduced in Baton Rouge in 1998 to help struggling single parents become first-time homeowners. The Warrick Dunn Foundation provides the down payment and works with area sponsors to furnish and equip the home with everything a family needs—from bed linens to appliances and food. "All they have to bring is their clothes," says Warrick.

"It was my mother's dream to own a home, but she never had that opportunity. So we want to live out that dream through others—taking a negative and turning it into a positive." The foundation has helped seventy-five parents and their nearly two hundred children realize the dream of homeownership. Currently, Homes operates in four cities: Baton Rouge, Tampa, Atlanta, and Tallahassee.

As I learned more about his work, I said to Warren, "What an amazing thing you're doing." He answered, "Thanks, Judge, but in my mind it's not amazing enough." For Warrick Dunn, "doing the best with what you've got" is a belief that propels him to acts of careful decision-making. Doing the best with what he's got enables him to do work that celebrates his mother's life, her dreams, and her memory.

Those of us who know Warrick Dunn personally are blessed with good fortune. We are delighted to witness his acts of love and kindness, to watch him play or play with him, to cheer for him—on field and off. In many ways, Warrick Dunn became the spiritual leader of the Atlanta Falcons. Many of his teammates told me stories of his kindness—of what a gentleman he is and how deeply he cares for his family.

Although he never sought the limelight, the spotlight often sought him, illuminating his kind ways and personal strength. Soon after he came to Atlanta, Warrick invited me to cochair a fund-raiser for his foundation, along with sports agent Leigh Steinberg. To be asked to be involved with his life-affirming organization was an honor and a treat.

As I grew to know Warrick over the years, I became more and more impressed. To this day, whenever I think of the Supreme Court Justice Thurgood Marshall's mantra "Do the best you can with what you've got," I think of Justice Marshall *and* of Warrick Dunn, the amazing running back and phenomenal young man, who I came to know well.

Warrick Dunn continues to bring honor to himself and his family. He rejoined the Tampa Bay Buccaneers, and off the field he has nurtured the foundation that means so much to him. His good works have not gone unnoticed. Warrick has been honored by the NFL with its Walter Payton Man of the Year Award, which recognizes excellence in community service and on the field.

Warrick has spearheaded league fund-raising for those in need. He joined a list that included Andre Agassi, Muhammad Ali, Alonzo Mourning, and Cal Ripken Jr. in founding Athletes for Hope. This charitable organization encourages athletes and the general public to become community volunteers.

Warrick has now retired from the NFL and is a part owner of the Atlanta Falcons NFL franchise. I am so proud of Warrick. He is a stand-up example of someone who did the best with what he had. He never lingered at any pity party, wishing things were different for him and his family. He didn't promise his siblings that he'd buy them a house when he finished college and hit it big in the NFL. He bought a house as soon as he possibly could. He marshaled the resources he had at the moment and moved definitively to make the best of the situation. He figured out what he could do with what he had right then and there. Warrick operates with a high sense of spiritual awareness too. He was able to meditate and decide matters in the way his mother taught him, in the way his mother would have. Warrick was able to see how it was possible to carry out his mother's dreams for her children. By tapping into his mother's teaching, by listening in the quiet for his mother's voice, he could see that, in a sense, his mother was preparing him for her death years before she left this world. The wisdom of the spirit is both a blessing and a grace.

Your goals may be different from those of Warrick Dunn, but if you do the best with what you've got, you can be effective. All of our dilemmas are personal; all of our challenges seem unique. But it is a general truth that doing the best with what you've got will solve many more problems than will mediocrity. Mediocrity certainly is in itself a problem.

Focus on Progress, Not on Lack

In order to do our very best, we have to be vigilant and careful not to focus exclusively on *what we lack*. So many of us can only seem to see or to talk about what we don't have, what we haven't gotten, what we wish we could have, or get, or be, or do. Surely, we are motivated to make progress by where we want to go, but in order to do our very best, we have to begin to observe and build on what we've already accomplished.

If you want a different or a better job, then focusing on the job you don't have won't move you any closer. Consider the job you do have, and articulate how you can move from where you are to where you'd like to go. If you want a better relationship with your spouse, or partner, or children, taking stock of the relationships you do have is the only way to begin to make change. If you focus only on what's absent from your relationships, if you consider only what these relationships lack, then you will be occupied with deficit thinking, and this kind of thinking won't move you any closer to what you want. We become what we think about. We produce what we think about. If we think about lack, that's what our thoughts will produce. If we think about our relationships, or our work, or our homes, then and only then do we have an opportunity to improve in these areas.

This approach is especially important with children. To encourage children, we have to be diligent about letting them know what they're doing right, what they're doing that we're proud of, what productive steps they're taking that we notice and can commend them for. To focus on what our children have not done, have not been able to accomplish, serves only to mire them in our disappointment. We don't want to distress our children by consistently presenting them with unmet expectations. Instead, we want to look at what they're doing well, or what they're doing at all, and help them redefine *their very best* based on what they're currently producing.

Psychologists, spiritualists, and high achievers agree that one of the key principles of life is this: what we think about expands. The images we hold in our minds are the realities that our subconscious seeks to produce for us. If we think about lack, we create more lack. If we want to gain ground, or attain new goals, or achieve new heights, we have to train ourselves to *see and think about what we want.* Thinking about what we don't have will only generate more of what we are thinking about—which is what we don't have.

Our very best is always a positive concept. Daring to do our very best is possible. When we work to do our very best, there is no room for lack in the actions we take. Work, doing our best, and taking productive action all involve using the tools, the materials, and the life we have before us. We can't improve on lack; we can't make anything better starting with what we don't have. What we can do is take what we have and move forward. What we can do is work with who we are, and improve ourselves in the ways we see fit. What we can do is encourage our children to do their very best, every time, and help them understand that as they get older, smarter, stronger, their very best changes with them.

Our very best begins with who we are already, and what we have already, and what we know already, and what we do today. This is what we have to build on. This is where we start on our journey forward.

Your Best Attention

Maybe your challenge is all about taking the best care you can of a disabled child. Or maybe troubling personal relationships or workplace stresses need your best attention. Maybe you need to change a persistently bad habit or to make lifestyle adjustments that will improve your health. Maybe you need to hold on to more of your money, or even some of your money.

Whatever challenges you face, no matter how tough it gets, ask yourself if you're doing the very best you can with what you've got. Your answer will either inspire you to persevere, or light a fire under you to offer more. We can all benefit from asking:

- Am I doing all I can for myself and those who depend on me?
- Am I maximizing my gifts, my talents, and my creativity?
- Am I reaching deep to face the hardest challenges?
- Am I remembering that every huge accomplishment is the sum of completing the simplest everyday demands?
- Am I doing my very best with the straightforward actions of the day?
- When I think I can do better, am I taking the critical step of applying what my mind is telling me to the actions in my daily life?

To accomplish one task allows us, and invites us, to move beyond that assignment. Once we complete a project, meet a goal, or even learn a lesson, our minds are primed for the next accomplishment. When our minds open up, our lives open up.

We go from one task to the next, whether we have done our very best or not. However, when we have done our *very* best, when we have used our minds as tools, and our hearts as guides, and our skills as fully as we are able, going from one task to the next becomes going from one achievement to the next. Doing our *very* best is an amazing and affirming experience every time.

What skills or interests or strengths do you have that you are not making full use of in your life? Do you complain more about what you do not have rather than be grateful for what you do have?

Doing your very best invites focus. Doing your very best invites you to assess for yourself when you're giving tasks your full attention, and when you're not. Doing your very best requires that you think first, and then take action, on purpose. Doing your very best brings your consciousness to all the small parts of what you're doing, so that small parts, well done, can add up to a much bigger accomplishment than what you would have achieved had you not done your *very* best at each step along the way.

Today:

Focus on the best of what you have to offer—not what you lack. Become determined to make the most of what you have. Today, I dare you to try and write down *all* of your blessings. Set a timer to be practical: see how many blessings you can list in five minutes!

Dare To...

Do your very best.

- Consider no action too small for your full attention.
- Take small steps and give even the smallest task your very best.

Experience how your life will change.

- Do your best to change your attitude if you tend to be negative.
- Give your household your best consistency and devotion.

Acknowledge when you are not doing your very best.

- Allow your understanding to trigger improvements.
- Stop being satisfied with using only half your energy or half your attention.

Seven

Recalculating Is Part of the Process

Plans are a way to navigate, to create that very important road map for where you're going. Once you've made a good plan, *working* your plan becomes critical to achieving your goal. Your plan will help you decide, at any given crossroads, which is the best way to go. After all, life constantly presents us with choices—good, bad, and neutral—and when we make new choices, new opportunities often present themselves.

While some of us were taught to plan from a very young age, apparently many of us were not.

Complex lives and higher goals require plans that are more definite and clear.

When we carefully and honestly assess what we define as important in life, we will uncover our life purpose. Defining our purpose equates with deciding what we want to invest in doing. *Defining our purpose is absolutely critical to good planning:*

- What are the specific tasks we're undertaking?
- Why are we doing what we've chosen to do?

Effective planning follows only when our purpose is clear:

- What do we need to do, to get what we want to do done?
- When can we set aside time to work on our tasks?
- When can we expect to finish?
- How much time do we need, or do we have, to do the task in front of us?
- Is the task or the goal so large that we need to make smaller tasks?

Our life options *always* improve when we plan our actions in advance. Carefully made plans that are aligned with our life purpose will serve as a road map to reaching our goals. In order to access the possibilities life offers us, *we believe we have to live according to our plan*. But plans are not set in stone.

Recalculating

Planning is an essential life skill that successful people cannot afford to be without. But often in our lives, we discover we're pursuing a direction just because we said we would, not necessarily because it's taking us where we want to go. Has this happened to you? It may be time to reconsider your approach.

A plan can be like a global positioning system, offering you the best route to take as you make your way to your destination. Global positioning systems have become commonplace these days and they help us find our way as we navigate. When I first got a GPS, I remember being amused and a bit amazed when I missed a turn and the voice inside my system announced that "he" was *recalculating* my route.

"Recalculate." This is not a very common term, but maybe recalculating should be a task we use for ourselves. If human beings learned how to recognize if and when we should recalculate, we'd be better off. If we got ourselves in the practice of recalculating, even as we pursue our plans, we'd be more flexible. We'd respond better to change. I've learned that being open to change can make a big positive difference in how we live and how we feel.

Notice I said "being open to change," not simply "changing." A disruption does not necessarily mean that our plans *need* changing. But when circumstances change, it is an opportunity to reconsider our plans. The light of our intelligence periodically needs to be brought to bear on what we're doing—especially when our circumstances shift. If going forward with the existing plan is the best strategy for our goals, then so be it. But if an opportunity or a change in circumstances brings along better opportunities, then recalculating may be in good order. New opportunities that serve our purpose are always worth examining.

Pursuing a plan can sometimes get in the way of the purpose you have in mind, because as we are pursuing our plans, our lives may change around us. Sometimes when life changes, our plans have to change, but we are—rightly—so busy bringing our plans to life that we fail to fully notice that our circumstances have shifted.

For a lifelong planner like me, this lesson is huge, and one I have been slow to accept. I did not like to get off my plan. I made my plans with too much care, and followed them diligently to create the life I wanted. For a long time, *anything* that took me off my plan was suspect.

Trying to figure out when to stay on the track we're on, and when to dare toward a destination that departs from our plans, can be daunting.

When conducting the business of life, it's not easy to recalculate. If you're a planner like me, you'll want to move along with dogged insistence, executing your plan. Most of us planners know that by adhering to our plan, we achieve results according to the goals that informed the plan in the first place.

Sometimes, however, we are presented with opportunities that *could not be on our plan*. At those times, recalculating not only makes sense, but is necessary. The challenge then becomes being able to recognize and respond to new opportunities or unexpected obstacles. Our task then becomes deciding whether to deviate from our plans, or figuring how to make new choices when we find ourselves at a crossroad.

Our plans are made to serve our purposes. Options that become available as we work toward our goals may serve our purpose better than what we are currently doing. We cannot plan for what we don't foresee. But we can have faith in the path we have chosen to take, and we can respond to the new opportunities that present themselves.

If I insisted on maintaining my plan no matter what, I would have missed more than one key opportunity in my lifetime.

Opportunity Demands Flexibility

When I was a young lawyer, I was hired by my dream employer, Delta Air Lines. I would serve as a litigator in the legal department at Delta's Atlanta headquarters.

These were high-flying days for the airlines. Federal deregulation had changed the face of the business. Delta had picked up some promising new routes and there was a great deal of excitement.

Rather than join a prominent law firm, I chose a corporate position because I thought it would be more manageable for me as a new mother. Make no mistake—this was in no way an easy job. In fact, being an in-house attorney for Delta was extremely demanding. The airline only had lawyers in Atlanta, which meant we were responsible for cases all over the country. Deciding to work in-house also mattered for our family: my husband at the time was a partner at a law firm, and I thought not working at competing firms would lend balance to our family while both of us practiced law.

My interest in Delta went beyond these considerations. I believed that if I did well, I could rise in the ranks to reach the level of senior attorney and become a corporate officer. I wanted to be positioned to be appointed to a board position. The board of directors has responsibility for the operations of the entire business worldwide. Even the chief executive officer (CEO) reports to the board of directors.

It all sounds pretty lofty, I'll admit. But I took the long view. I had adopted my parents' mantra that my brothers and I "could be anything we wanted." Setting up my plans to help me achieve my dreams is what I have always done, and still do.

I joined Delta as the company's highest-ranking woman of color. I was proud and excited, and I was working like crazy. I don't have to tell those of you who are working parents about the balancing act! Doing the best we can for our families while doing the best we can on the job—this is our challenge, our constant struggle.

All the while, I worked to be a good spouse, to care for my six-month-old son, to maintain some level of community service, and to find a little time and space for myself.

Although things were going well for me, by mid-decade my employer was experiencing tough times. There was a horrific crash of a Delta L-1011 jetliner while approaching a runway at the Dallas–Fort Worth airport; tragically, 133 people were killed. The crash was attributed to wind shear. Amazingly, thirty people survived. Then a few years later, in a crazy irony, another plane crashed in Dallas. This time fourteen people lost their lives.

A *Change of Course*

I remember clearly the wave of disbelief that washed over our office as the news hit. Coming so soon on the heels of the first crash and at the same airport, it just seemed unreal, although, sadly, it was not. People were dead, and we had to respond. Anticipating that I would be dispatched to the Dallas–Fort Worth airport the day of the crash, I hurried to meet some needed deadlines and was on my way home to pack when my office phone rang.

I answered, breathless and a bit dazed. It was my boss and he was not sending me to Texas. Much to my surprise, he asked me to report across the street to the corporate media relations department where I was being temporarily reassigned to deal with the aftermath of the crash. It was a stressful and challenging time. In a crisis, one of the most important duties of a corporation is to provide the media with accurate, thorough information. Even though there were not nearly as many media outlets as there are today, my new team and I were kept busy feeding information to aggressive reporters. Because there were so many complex legal matters involved, it made sense to bring in a lawyer who could directly answer relevant questions.

The day after Flight 1141 crashed, Flight 1141 departed Dallas–Fort Worth and skidded off the runway—in the same airport, at the same scheduled time. *On the very next day.* The chances of this happening are *so* remote. A coincidence of the worst kind. This of course sent the press into their own tailspin of calls and inquiries. When one of the wire services drilled me about the incident, I answered honestly. "Look," I said, "I just put my two young sons and their nanny on a Delta jet this morning to their grandmother's house in Ohio because I'm working around the clock and need someone to look after them. If I had any question at all about the capacity of the people flying those planes, no child of mine would be flying! These boys are the most precious thing in my life and I trust any one of the pilots wearing a Delta uniform to get them where they're going." Of course, I answered as a mother and as a Delta senior attorney—my job was to address the questions and the panic of the hour.

I remained in the media relations office for about a week. When the immediate flurry was over, I returned to the law department and my regular duties, including preparing for a large, multimillion-dollar antitrust case. A few days later I took a call informing me that my boss, who oversaw both the legal and public relations departments, wanted to see me immediately.

As I raced upstairs, all kinds of (mostly negative) possibilities flew through my head—maybe I hadn't been diplomatic enough when dealing with the press. Perhaps I had been quoted out of context in presenting the company's positions. Had my responding as a lawyer, and as a mother, been too much? I breathed deeply and presented myself at Jim's office.

"Close the door, please, Glenda," he instructed. As I took the seat across from him, I was downright worried. This couldn't be good.

The short version of the story is that I had *not* screwed up and my temporary assignment was very well received. As a result, Jim explained that he wanted to permanently reassign me to handle the media. This struck me as surprising, even ridiculous. As politely as possible I suggested as much. "Jim, this is a flattering offer, but I'm a lawyer. I don't know the first thing about press relations and I'm in the middle of some really big cases."

What I didn't say to Jim, but what I really meant, was that this was not part of my plan. In fact, it was a pretty significant departure from "My Big Life Plan," and I didn't want to hear a word about it. For seven years, the plan had been my blueprint. Believing that I knew where I was heading held me together when things got crazy. And certainly there had been plenty of crazy along the way.

Jim was kind. He praised my performance in the aftermath of the crash and said that if I could do so well with no training or preparation, surely I could contribute significantly to the company's media relations efforts.

"I so appreciate what you're saying and the generous offer, Jim, but this just isn't my world. Media is not what I was trained to do. The press plays by a whole different set of rules than lawyers do. Sometimes, it seems like the press doesn't have any predictable rules at all. Thanks anyway, but I'd much prefer to stay where I am." Jim urged me to discuss this with my then husband. He also encouraged me to *keep my mind open*. I didn't think there was much to think or talk about, but I consented to his wishes.

As I turned to leave the office, Jim fired off this bombshell: "Glenda, I just want you to know that the president and the chairman of the board have asked that you make this move."

Within seconds, and with trepidation, I realized that the decision had been made for me. This last announcement changed the climate in the room. Yes, I was being asked to "consider" taking the media job, but I understood that when the president and the chairman of the board have "asked," now, that is a different proposition.

The alignment of my own personal inner system shifted. My mind raced as I tried to mentally justify such a move. True, I would not be working as a litigator, but I would remain at Delta. And even though I would be stepping somewhat away from the plan, I could still achieve my goals within the company. If my goal was a long-term career with

Delta, which of course it was, I would have to accept a position for which I had been handpicked by the chief executives. That's just the way corporate America works.

I took a breath and asked Jim, "Well, when do you want me to move?" Then I jokingly added, "Would right after lunch be soon enough?"

The new work proved to be both amazing and fascinating. At that time, airline hijackings were a near-constant threat, and my pager was on 24/7—even in church, thanks to the "vibrate" mode. Responding to and staying ahead of the media was a huge amount of pressure and was a significant contribution to the company.

Our office was the public face of Delta Air Lines, and I personally was responsible for fifty domestic cities, and all of Europe and Asia. We had a huge job to do. I worked hard and came to enjoy this very challenging work. Ultimately, work with the media exposed me to opportunities and to people that would never have come my way as a litigator.

Handling media for Delta was a new option I could not have planned for that came my way while I was working my plan. Being successful at this new assignment meant that I had accomplished a course correction. Ultimately, I began to feel really good about not just being able to do the job, but also about being capable of adjusting my plan to fit my opportunities. I missed litigating, but I was happy in media relations and continued to rise up the ladder of the organization.

The Judge

A couple of years later, Judge Romea Turner Powell passed away. A longtime civil rights advocate and a family friend, Judge Powell sat on the Fulton County Juvenile Court for more than twenty years. I knew and followed her work, respected her tremendously, and loved her as a person. Her passing was a personal loss for me, and as it turned out, she had plans that would be critically important to my future.

Two months before her death, Judge Powell called me from what I later learned was her hospital room. I knew she had slowed down, but I did not know, nor did she let on, how sick she really was. I assumed she was at home but was just not feeling her best.

When her call came, it was a Saturday morning in May. Miraculously, my house was empty and quiet. Typically I wasn't at home on Saturdays, but on this particular morning the boys were out with their father. I was able to be focused and very present for this conversation.

Judge Powell chatted with me about life and the family, and I realized that it was quite out of character for her to speak in this relaxed way. Our conversations were usually very short and to the point. I now see that being at home and being open to her call was a blessing, and was meant to happen.

We continued chatting, and then she abruptly changed the subject. "Glenda," she asked, "what would it take to get you to leave Delta?"

Delta was my company; I had never considered leaving. There were lots of pluses for me there, including the fact that my family and I could fly anywhere, anytime. Having access and opportunity to see other parts of the world was a big benefit of working so hard at Delta. Once my mom and I escaped for a last-minute getaway to Athens, Greece. When our appetite for adventure wasn't quite satisfied, I said, "Mom, what would you think about a couple of days in Cairo?" We had both always wanted to see the pyramids, and that's exactly what we did! Within a couple of hours we were on a jet and on our way. Delta was making possible a wonderful lifestyle for me and my family.

Feeling quite comfortable with a woman I'd known most of my life, I told Judge Powell honestly about my plans, and how Delta was the perfect professional home for me. With no idea that she was so sick, I didn't really grasp at that moment that she was feeling me out as her possible replacement. I listened as Judge Powell told me about her work—how fulfilling it was and how she loved engaging with kids and families. I admitted it sounded interesting, but not for me. What's more, *I had a plan.*

After her passing I was quite surprised to learn that Judge Powell had conveyed to her husband and a professional confidant that she hoped I would apply for the job as her successor on the juvenile court bench.

But a colleague of Judge Powell's called and urged me to meet with him. I asked my father to sit in on the meeting. After it was over Daddy quietly said to me, "Glenda, I know you do not see this as part of your path, but I think it is important that you take the time to really consider it. Promise me you'll keep it in mind for a few days. Pray about it and see what happens."

As always, I took my father's suggestions quite seriously. I laugh today as I remember a series of "yo-yo" prayers in which I alternately beseeched and challenged God. "Dear Lord, you don't want me to give up this incredible job and lifestyle, do you? It's what I've always wanted and I'm really doing well here."

Then from the other side of my brain came, "God, is this an opportunity to step out and really make a difference? Are you calling me? Is this something you want me to do? Help!"

Of course I could never replace the opportunities and perks Delta generously offered. I could not jet around the world for free on a moment's notice. There was so much else that I would miss if I left Delta. But what I slowly permitted to enter my consciousness was what I could do as a juvenile court judge. I was a mother, I had always loved children, and I came from solid family values. Beyond that, a decade in the trenches of corporate America convinced me that I could be tough and was capable of making tough decisions.

Despite strong doubts, I still felt the need to fill out an application for the appointment. After completing the application, I held on to it until the deadline day. I could not let myself turn it in unless I was absolutely certain that I would say yes if appointed.

Glenda the planner kept insisting, *But what about the plan?* I had no idea where this job would lead, but the more I thought and the more I prayed, the more I was able to separate myself from my plan and see the amazing opportunity before me to be of service. After much consideration, I began to see that allegiance to my plan was hindering my progress.

The more I thought about it, the more I realized that if I were ever going to take such a step outside the plan, this was a step worth taking. On the juvenile court bench, I could make a sustainable difference. Once I turned in that application, I was fully committed. Believe me, I never thought I would do anything but "follow the plan," but after prayer and struggle, I concluded that it was time to "recalculate." This change of course put me in alignment with my life's passion. Finally, I dared to open myself to the possibilities.

I later learned there were sixty-three candidates for the position. From that large pool, I was appointed to the bench. There certainly were some heavy hitters in that group and I was honored to be chosen.

The lesson was huge. Once a planner always a planner, that's true. But today I do not plan with such insistence—I am more open to the need for adjustment than ever before. And now, being able to recognize when life is calling on me to adjust—well, I've gotten good at that. I'm comfortable making course corrections now.

*   *   *

To this day I have no idea where I will be in five years, or ten years, or, God only knows, after retirement. What I do know is that my work on the juvenile court, combined with my media work, combined with my training in the law, led to my TV show. Being on plan, and being willing to go off plan, gave me a tremendous opportunity to share my passion and concern for children and families with millions of people.

Stubbornly insisting on my plan would have kept me moving toward the goals I had identified, but would also have prevented me from the work I now know to be my life's calling.

I could not be more grateful that I dared to depart from my ironclad plan. To listen to Judge Powell, to take counsel with my father, to pray, to fill out the application, to finally turn it in—these were all smaller steps that I took trying to gradually consider the all-important question: Is this a time to recalculate? Is this a time to make a new plan that includes a new starting point? Is it time for me to take the life I have made, the skills I have, and dare to go in a new direction?

The truth is, life offers more than one way to support our purpose. And as our lives evolve, our sense of purpose also evolves. If we choose to marry and have children, our lives change greatly, and our purposes also change. We have gone from investing fully in our careers, to building a life with a spouse, to being the primary protectors and teachers of children. If we decide to change careers, or we decide to start a business, we shift our attention from maintaining our performance level to gearing up for making new impressions and focusing on direct interaction with customers or clients. Although purpose and planning are intertwined, they can also come unraveled. I'm glad to have learned this lesson. Sometimes, the change of course that presents itself to us is too important to be avoided. Some choices are so unexpected, and so positive, that even though we could not have planned for it, the choice supports our ultimate goal, and is worth pursuing.

Learning this lesson has helped me make better decisions at some challenging crossroads in my own life. Being confident enough about what I have achieved according to my plan, and being flexible enough to take advantage of new options—these are the life skills that come with being a good planner and living according to the blueprint you've set for yourself. You realize that you have been traveling the right path, and that the new choice before you—that you could not have foreseen—comes as the grace of good fortune. Being on the right road offers options that the wrong road may not.

Think about your own path for a moment. Can you picture a time when you moved forward somewhat blindly? Have you ever just refused to adjust? Have you ever been unwilling to reconsider what you planned in light of other options—and then possibly regretted that refusal later?

Today:

Consider whether there is something in your personal or professional life that needs to be recalculated. Within the next ninety minutes outline the recalculation plan.

Dare To...

Make a plan, even if it is the first large-scale plan you've ever made.

- If you are not currently a planner, take advantage of giving your life a blueprint. Do it now.
- Decide on your current purpose(s), and list the work you need to do to reach your goal.
- Once you've made your plan, align your actions every day to achieving it. Or as the saying goes, "Plan your work and work your plan."

Recalculate, when options for change present themselves.

- When new opportunities arise, consider them, and do so carefully. If an option presents itself that you could not have imagined, be ready to make a new plan, to support an opportunity that furthers your purposes and excites your mind.

Be in control.

- Control your efforts and your time.
- Don't give your life over to chance. Give your life over to planning with flexibility, and then watch how your chances improve.

Eight

Get Real About Reality

Our lives are shaped, or misshaped, by what we choose to convince ourselves of. Far too many of us live our lives as we wish they were, rather than deal with the reality we are presented with. This can often happen when those closest to us fall short of our expectations. Where we are able, some of us choose to live a kind of parallel existence where we don't have to face reality. If we choose to ignore what confronts us, then reality ultimately catches up to us. It's our choice whether to turn and face what we know to be real or try to keep running away until we get caught.

This idea of "getting caught" by reality is not positive. In the best of worlds, our realities would not be conditions that we want to run from. But this book is in part about overcoming hard times. What I know from experience in my life, and with my friends and family, is this: ignoring the truth *creates* hard times. Confronting the truth, and managing your reality, *empowers you* to shape a life that you don't need to run from.

When we don't face and don't handle the truth about the people in our lives, our lives get off balance. We get out of control, and our dreams get further out of reach. Our children do get involved in things we don't want them to. Our affairs get out of order. When we are careless about facing and handling the truth of our lives, then we begin to run from our reality. Not facing the truth makes you a ducker, a dodger, a drone. Every person who refuses to face the truth is a person who doesn't realize that reality *will* respond to your handling. This applies to how we respond to how the people in our lives treat (or mistreat) us and others. You may not be able to control the actions of another, but you *can* control how you respond. We make our lives—once we have control of them. Our lives do not make us.

We hang on to destructive relationships sometimes with spouses, friends, colleagues, and even family members. We fail to open up honest dialogue that could unleash the truth. Honesty would probably improve these relationships and make them work better for us. In some cases facing the truth can mean facing the end of a relationship, and that's where it really gets tough.

Each one of us has authentic needs, which cannot be ignored without greatly diminishing the quality of our lives. I knew two women who I wish understood the need for all of us to know what's real for us. Rebecca and Michelle avoided the truth about the people closest to them for so long that both their lives were derailed, and both of them gave up their goals and plans.

Truth and Friendship

Rebecca and I shared the personality trait that we always held a clear vision for our lives. Our visions were different, but we both knew what we wanted and we both aimed for our goals. Rebecca always envisioned herself a wife and mother. So while we were both maturing and educating ourselves, she was looking for the proverbial "Mr. Right." When she met Henry, the man of her dreams, her plans kicked into full gear.

As her husband built a career and developed prominence in their Midwest community, Rebecca built a social network that fostered major connections and brought forth the "right" invitations. As a couple, they were handsome and popular. They attended all the right parties. Rebecca proved to be a huge asset to her husband's business affairs. This was the role she imagined for herself, and so she and her husband were in agreement that she was playing a role they both wanted and benefited from.

When their children came along, Rebecca wanted for nothing. Their children were beautiful, smart and accomplished, athletic, and in private school, of course. Rebecca became the perfect soccer mom, drove a minivan for her children's carpool, delivered their children to music lessons, and with plenty of help at home hosted lots of dinner parties. She had an extensive wardrobe and a house "to die for."

Of course, all that glitters is not gold. Sadly, life inside the walls of their beautifully decorated suburban home was a mess for Rebecca and her children. This family of privilege and prestige was caught up in a family drama that none of us could see. Their family problems unfolded innocuously enough. Rebecca's dream husband had a temper. And Rebecca, in her single-minded pursuit of her goal, neither wanted to admit this to herself nor acknowledge it to others.

Over time, Rebecca's husband's fussy displays gave way to occasional episodes of verbal abuse. Ultimately, I learned that Henry not only started to scream at her, but also began insulting her, calling her stupid and telling her she was a lousy mother and wife. His insults were completely false. As I've said, Rebecca handled the children well, managed his household at the level of their income, and worked hard to become an asset to his business. After insulting her, he would apologize—bring flowers, buy gifts—and she would accept his contrition.

But the patterns of verbal abuse persisted, and the cycle escalated. Many victims of abuse have experienced this same sickening pattern. The episodes became more frequent, the volume of his tirades increased, and the drama intensified. Like so many other victims of abuse, Rebecca chose not to process this treatment as abusive. No matter how loud or nasty he got, Henry would ultimately apologize, beg forgiveness, and treat her with post-rage tenderness.

While the abuse was ongoing and the cycle was escalating, Rebecca did not reach out for help. She had a big problem. By making a soccer mom of herself—by limiting her activities to her husband's business and their children's school-related activities—she was totally dependent on this increasingly out-of-control, abusive husband. Both of them participated in a horrible charade, continuing to appear for all the world like the perfect couple. They were perfectly imperfect, and hiding all they could. Because her husband's behavior did not fit Rebecca's plan, she denied the struggle she faced and tried to keep going, wearing her game face.

You know the next chapter to this story. Eventually, lashing out verbally no longer satisfied Henry. Without anyone to stop him, he began lashing out physically: hitting Rebecca with his fists or with the back of his hand. Rebecca went from being insulted and screamed at to being hit or slapped. The presence of their children did not stop him.

Rebecca refused to tell her friends and family about the abuse. She began to wear telltale sunglasses and tried to hide her bruises with makeup. Instead of reaching out, she chose, as so many victims do, to isolate herself and her children from others. Rebecca thought that by hiding, she would keep others from figuring out what was going on.

The embarrassment she would face if anyone knew the real story was more than she thought she could bear. She thought she would be better off living with the deteriorated marriage, since this marriage and the progress she had made were central to her life plan. With everything crumbling around her, to take a new path seemed like the wrong move.

But facing reality is always the right move.

Rebecca started to crumble. The stress took a toll on her health—her blood pressure rose to a dangerous level and her self-esteem dipped to a dangerous low. She stubbornly refused to admit that this could happen to her. After all, she had married the perfect guy and they were creating the life of her dreams. This was the man who would make her plan work—he would care for her and she would stay home. The two of them would attain popularity and prominence; life would be perfect for them and for their children.

Henry's abuse of Rebecca was not his only problem. Because Rebecca focused on their social network and their household, she went about her days blithely unaware of the issues developing in Henry's business dealings. For years he had been involved in embezzling funds from wealthy clients, quietly reinvesting the money in questionable operations. As the authorities closed in on Henry and his scheme, his violence at home escalated. He would soon hit rock bottom.

To her credit, Rebecca did not stand still, so she and her children were gone by the time the law came for Henry. Despite her longing to maintain her comfortable lifestyle, she finally realized that there was no way the marriage could continue. She had begun to fear for her life and for the lives of her children. One night, unable to compromise her and her children's safety any longer, she packed a small suitcase, took the little bit of cash she could lay her hands on, and escaped her violent husband. She and her children made their way to a motel, conditions that were a far cry from the life she knew.

At this point, Rebecca, who knew nothing of the extent of her husband's problems at work, believed Henry's situation was just a temporary setback. She assumed she would soon be able to get legal protection, that she and the children would move back to their house, and that Henry would be required to move out. In the meantime, she had to acknowledge that because of her fear of the truth, her "life plan" had turned into a completely undesirable situation. Not facing the truth had turned a good life to hard times.

Rebecca left the motel and found a short-term furnished apartment for herself and the kids. She assumed that within the month she would file divorce proceedings. But before she could execute the next step in her plan, Henry was indicted.

All hell broke loose. The bank accounts were frozen, and basically everything the family had was seized.

With this intervention by legal authorities, Rebecca's safety net disappeared. All the material and marital privileges of her life were gone: the car, the furnishings, the vacations, and the image of the perfect family. Talk about having to recalculate!

Rebecca was forced to dig deep, and to tell herself the hard truth. Here's what she said to me: "I finally realized that my dream for my life had turned into a nightmare. I knew one of two things could happen. I could continue to live in that nightmare, and possibly die, *and* put my children at incredible risk. Or I could be open to another possibility."

Rebecca completed the education she had abandoned, got a job, and did what was necessary to get on her feet and provide for her children.

Ultimately, Rebecca had to abandon the plan she made for herself. But she stalled; she refused to "face the music" until she was brought to the brink of catastrophe. I hope you've never had an experience remotely similar, but I think we all can learn from her experience.

Rebecca acknowledged that for some people, the recognition that their master plan was leading nowhere would have come sooner. But she was as invested in her vision as anyone could be, and the possibility that her family and her future were disintegrating was an extremely hard reality to face.

Rebecca's story is an extreme example of what can happen when our plans outlive their purposes, and when we resist reality, even when reality stands up and shouts. Further, it serves as a reminder—maybe even a wake-up call—that sometimes the reality of life requires that we develop a new plan or change course. It is not wise to keep following a plan that's going nowhere.

Michelle failed to face her reality as well, although hers is a very different story. I had known Michelle for years. She attended private schools and earned a degree from one of the best-known Ivy League colleges. But in my humble opinion, those and other blessings were taken for granted. Michelle proved herself basically lazy and unmotivated. She preferred being taken care of to working. She made sure she found someone to take care of her at every juncture of her life. After exhausting her parents' generosity, she sought out and found Rob, a promising physician and the perfect husband—or at least a husband perfectly able to provide for her.

Unfortunately, beginning early in the marriage, Rob felt the need to have sex with many, many other women, or so the story went. Michelle chose to ignore Rob's flagrant philandering because she didn't want to lose all the trappings of her lavish lifestyle. They had a palatial home in California, took many trips, and owned multiple cars.

Even after the birth of their four sons, Michelle's husband continued to step out on her. After each dalliance was discovered, Rob would apologize and come up with another extravagant "forgive me" gift. Michelle's collection of diamonds grew, so she looked the other way. But Michelle and Rob were far from content. Her marriage was a sham by any estimation. Although she had four great kids, she had not grown personally as an adult.

Michelle seemed to think that the issues in her marriage were not visible. But I and others of her friends could see that she was trading self-respect for shelter and glam. Despite my concern about her patterns of dependence, and her seeming inability to see what was clear to everyone else, she and I maintained a friendship over the years. Like everyone, she complained once in a while. When she invited a response to her situation, to her complaints, I suggested that her unhappiness might be a result of her own choices. Even in the midst of everything that was going on in her life, Michelle insisted on living a lie. She constantly stated, almost like a mantra, that her marriage was strong and that her husband loved her dearly. Most of us looking in saw it differently.

Michelle had been given many opportunities. Yet she had not taken any initiative to make a life *for herself*. She was unable to face her own truth: she could not accept that her husband was philandering, that her marriage was in a shambles, and that she had traded disrespect on her husband's part for a comfortable life. By not facing her own reality, she lived in denial. This continued even after Michelle was divorced, when she made every attempt to find others to "fix" her problems. To me she was a victim of her own greed and her refusal to be a self-starter. She resisted the plain truth that we all need to be self-sufficient, a mistake for which she paid a very high price.

I'm not sure whether Michelle failed to understand or believe that she was capable. What I do know was that all her friends and supporters knew she was competent. Michelle absolutely failed to live up to her God-given abilities. She spent all her adult life depending on others, which did not in any measure reflect the honest truth of her skills or her needs.

I don't think I was tactless with Michelle; I never spoke to her as bluntly as I am writing about her here. Instead, I tried gently yet strongly to encourage her to figure out what would satisfy her soul. This helpless persona she had created had not gotten her far, and would not serve her well in the future.

Michelle did not take my advice, and may not have heard or understood me. Years went by, and nothing much changed for her. Once their four children were out of the house, Rob decided there was little left for him in this marriage of convenience, and he left. Facing the end of a lifestyle, Michelle was depressed and a little bit desperate. This wasn't how she pictured her midlife years.

Michelle fell victim to her own sense of entitlement, and to her husband's dangerous infidelity. Her hesitation or refusal to seek self-reliance created a lot of the disappointment she faced. She had so much going for her, but she did not identify how she needed to improve her life or her lot. Without deciding where she wanted to go, what she wanted to do, she remained adrift, without purpose and without a viable plan. Without acknowledging that she needed to make some decisions, that she needed to take action to shape her own life, Michelle floundered, hesitated, and let too much time go by without acting on her own strength. She behaved as if a knight in shining armor would rescue her from adult responsibilities. For many years, Rob provided for her and their children, even though Michelle put up with quite a bit as the children were growing. After Rob filed for divorce, Michelle ended up with a settlement that was adequate but certainly did not afford her the lifestyle to which she was accustomed.

Even though I deeply questioned how she handled herself, I reached out to her and tried to offer some support.

One of my gifts is helping people make connections that can help them move forward. After the divorce, I connected Michelle with another friend of mine who owned a service business. I expected that Michelle would find a niche in this company. After meeting her, the owner agreed with me.

Although she never really wanted to, Michelle took the job. But she had never wanted any job or any trappings of responsibility. After she accepted the job, she behaved illogically and unpredictably. Her performance in the new position was dismal. She embarrassed herself and me. This business owner was someone with whom I also had a long friendship—someone who trusted my opinion. Eventually, I had to apologize. He had done me a huge favor by even considering Michelle. I had wasted his time, energy, and resources. I also probably damaged his trust in me. What's more, he had decided on someone else for the job before my call about Michelle came in. Against his better judgment, but out of respect for me, he gave Michelle the opportunity and lost a much better candidate. Somehow, he did not hold it against me and remains a good friend. I think he witnessed Michelle sabotage her own chances at success.

Michelle also behaved as if no one had gone out on a limb for her. I have rarely encountered a person who behaved so much as if supporting herself was not something she needed to take seriously. Michelle did not do her part to manage her own life. The truth is that each of us is much better off if we make use of all the skills God gives us. Pretending that we can't diminishes us and moves us farther away from the spiritual honesty that's necessary for fulfillment and joy.

Michelle created a long-term pity party at which she was the honored guest. She blamed her husband and anyone else she could for her changed circumstances. Let me be clear—her husband was hardly innocent and had behaved totally inappropriately in his marriage. But he moved on. He remarried and moved to another city, while remaining close with their four adult children.

When we talked during that period, Michelle rarely used the word "I." Instead the discussion focused on Rob—where Rob chose to live, who Rob married, the money Rob was not sharing with her, etc. "Rob did thus and so to me." An endless tape ran through her mind and out of her mouth—everything was all about everybody else. Michelle kept herself fully engaged with the past. Rob's moving on had shown that the past was over. But this was not true for Michelle, because of the "tapes" she played in her head.

The truth will set you free.

Do you think Michelle could have changed her mantra if she had somehow been made to understand how self-destructive her pattern had become? I'm not sure. She never wanted to acknowledge the truth that her life was her responsibility. Midlife is nowhere near too late to make productive choices. Many mothers with college-age children turn in their minivan keys and go forward with the rest of their lives.

People certainly tried to help Michelle recalibrate her thinking. There was no reason she had to be so backward-looking, and so bereft of the material things she had come to appreciate. After many years of observing her, I do not think any of us could have altered things for her. Her goals needed to arise from within—inside her soul, her personality, her intentions for herself.

Michelle needed to become much more of a self-starter, to take more initiative, to find gainful, fulfilling employment, to concentrate on herself and not on her former husband. She never changed. But the end did come and I had to let our friendship go.

We have to surround ourselves with people who support our perspectives. Friendship is too delicate to maintain a poor fit.

Michelle proved herself a person who couldn't get out of her own way. She blamed everything and everybody for her situations.

I have learned in my life to try to surround myself with positive, motivated people who inspire me to do my best. Michelle had not fit the bill for a long time, but after a while it became clear that she would continue to remain victimized. She would not adjust her limiting vision of herself or of her abilities, and so she proved herself a person who will never really change. She remained stuck in place, still looking for a knight in shining armor to come and rescue her.

It is important to me to achieve what I set out to do. I fully intend, and do everything I can, to align my life so that I can pursue my dreams. To watch these two women sacrifice their desires out of some misguided notion that the truth could be avoided—well, I'll just admit that watching this was very difficult for me.

I cannot say I know exactly what Rebecca's or Michelle's dreams actually were. I do know that, in my humble estimation, both of them lived in a fantasy world. Rebecca's dream to be well-regarded and a good mother and an affluent wife was achieved, but could not be maintained because of her abusive husband and her crumbling, unsupportive marriage.

Michelle, on the other hand, needed tough love. She needed to realize that you get from life what you put into it. Because she wouldn't address the truth, even to be willing to say out loud what she needed or what she didn't have, she led herself to a place where she couldn't even enjoy life.

Running from or hiding from reality is not unusual. We are conditioned to believe that reality is difficult, and so we may behave as if the truth is safe to avoid. Too many people will choose the easy way out. Too many people don't acknowledge that the way to go is in!

I'm here to tell you that we don't *really* have a choice about whether to accept reality, whether to act on what we know to be so.

The Parent Trap

Our children can lead us into self-deception as well. When we don't see the truth about our children, we can get caught in a parent trap. We love our children and go to great lengths for them. Yet sometimes our concern and our desire to protect our children can lead to self-deception. Sometimes parents cross a line with their children, and a desire to protect them blinds them to their bad behavior.

We all know a child who seems obnoxious to everyone else yet is considered darling by her doting parents. The child is in no way easy to be with, but her parents refuse to view her whining and tantrums with any level of objectivity. Truth is, parents are sometimes unable, as well as unwilling, to see. They're deceiving themselves because they don't want to face the implication or accusation that they are weak or indulgent parents. They perceive a failing that they don't want to face.

A successful physician appeared in my juvenile courtroom with his teenage son. His son had been brought before the law because he had been involved in a number of scrapes. The seriousness of his actions had been slowly escalating.

The son, an upper-middle-class teen, had been out joyriding with his friends. They were bored, were looking for something to do, and had too much time and money. Translation: they were heading for trouble.

In the past the teenager and his friends had been involved in annoying pranks that were bothersome but that didn't do much harm. This time was different. Carrying a shotgun pilfered from his dad's "locked" gun cabinet, the physician's son and his unarmed friends quite literally shot their way into the home of another boy their age. "It was a joke," the boy told me in court. "We were just messing around, we never meant to hurt anybody. We knew the people who lived there were out of town."

Apparently proud of their misbehaviors, these youngsters foolishly bragged about their exploit to friends at school.

I was fed up with this spoiled-brat scenario and issued a sentence of eighty hours of community service, which can take a teenager who is in school roughly ten weeks to complete. In this teenager's case, a few days in jail would not have been one bit out of line. But I opted for community service, hopeful that spending some time among people less fortunate might have the desired effect on this teen.

The boy listened quietly, looking appropriately humbled. His father, on the other hand, shot up from his seat with great indignation.

"No way, Judge!" he exclaimed. "There's absolutely no way—this sentence should be no more than ten hours. No child of mine is going to be spending eighty hours at some dangerous inner-city project!" This father, so used to controlling everybody and everything in his world, had dared to challenge what I knew to be a very lenient sentence. I should have held him in contempt at that point, but I was curious to see how outrageous he intended to be. This was a parent clearly caught in a trap: he wanted to believe, and also apparently wanted me to believe, that his son was doing no serious harm, that he deserved no solid punishment.

The doctor saw fit to recommend an appropriate sentence to me. He believed his son should do ten hours of community service, in the hospital where he was on staff! So not only was he completely lying to himself about his kid's behavior, he was trying to soften the blow by giving his son a make-work job that he would oversee!

Of course, the time when it was this parent's job to correct his son's behavior and lay out consequences for his actions had passed. His son was now in court, which meant his actions had escalated beyond the parent's sole control.

My response was swift and straightforward. "All right, sir. If you think eighty hours is inappropriate, hear this. In lieu of holding you in contempt and citing you for your unnecessary outburst, I have amended your son's sentence to 120 hours of community service, which you and your son will participate in jointly, at a location selected by this court!" I banged my gavel and sat back in my seat, rather pleased with myself.

The father turned to his lawyer and shrieked, "Do something!" I glared at the lawyer as he rose from his seat, preparing to speak. My raised eyebrow seemed to encourage the lawyer to reconsider. "Your Honor, 120 hours is accepted," the lawyer said.

Talk about self-deception. This father, with no apparent sense of boundaries when it came to his son, was living a lie of significant and destructive proportions. Not only was he unable to imagine that his child was capable of the actions he was clearly taking, but in the face of cold, hard facts the father refused to acknowledge the truth. In his mind's eye—I guess I should say *in his mind's lie*—his son could do no wrong.

Parents are in the special situation of being in charge of others' lives. This means that parents' self-deception not only affects adults, but can also involve the children they have responsibility for. The truth we don't see can hurt children too. Some parents simply refuse to see what's going on in front of their noses. They abdicate responsibility by giving too much leeway to babysitters. They believe handing over the keys to a car is a substitute for spending time with a teen. They dole out credit cards before teaching responsibility, believing they are being generous when instead they are being foolish.

When we lie to ourselves as parents, we can actually get our kids into trouble too. We have a job to do, communicating expectations and setting limits for our children. When we give them credit cards and don't teach them about money, we have deceived ourselves that they will understand by magic, and we have done them a disservice. When we leave their teaching to others—caretakers, teachers, even grand-parents—we deceive ourselves that they will absorb our principles and our values without our spending sufficient time with them. We become disappointed in what our children do or don't do, without giving them the opportunity to do what we've modeled or explained. When we fail to set limits for our children, or to provide adequate consequences for their behavior, we deceive ourselves into thinking that they will do right with-out instruction or monitoring, and we don't give them the grace of being corrected in a safe space, by people who love them unconditionally. We allow them to misbehave, and they repeat those poor choices until some of them are confronted with the law. In court, they are confronted with the harsh realities of the consequences of their behavior.

Another young man I faced in court was charged with breaking and entering his girlfriend's apartment and beating her. This young man's mother insisted that the girlfriend had provoked her innocent son.

In fact, the son was already on probation for other very serious charges. His mother was blinded by her own internal lies to the real and present danger facing her son. For this mother, as well as for the physician discussed earlier, facing the truth would have meant facing their own failures. And you and I both know that dropping the ball on this most important task in our lives—raising our children—is not something easily acknowledged. We all have personal failures, some minor, some major. The problem is that if we lie to ourselves, our fail-ures can grow from small to large, because we refuse to face the truth. The lies we tell ourselves, like all the seeds that take root in our spirits, ultimately not only guide our thoughts but also influence our actions. The truth hurts, the old adage warns, but the outcome of lying can hurt worse than the truth.

Lies find their way into even the most loving of environments. A friend of mine grew up in a warm household with loving, caring parents. His siblings grew into productive adults. My friend, however, is an alcoholic—smart and high-performing but intoxicated about 75 percent of his waking hours. In retrospect, this upstanding family probably lied to themselves, refusing to acknowledge his problem, which they probably could see was getting worse.

Alcoholism was not part of this family's self-image. They missed or ignored the warning signs and kept hoping the problems would go away. Typical teenage experimentation, they told themselves when we were younger. My friend's parents reprimanded him, but they believed the behavior would end. It did not. By the time they acknowledged what was really going on, my friend was, as an adolescent, even more deeply into substance abuse. These parents had simply refused to come to grips with the facts.

My friend slipped through the cracks because everyone was lying to themselves about the seriousness of the situation. As a result he faced a lifetime of struggle that possibly could have been averted.

Everybody and their mama can do what's easy in life, according to my Aunt Frances. The difference between surviving and thriving can be seen by looking at who takes it easy versus who knows what is real. Life takes work, energy, diligence, devotion, honesty. Life is not easy, so why pretend? Just because life is not easy does not mean that a good life is impossible. We've got to live to our fullest potential. Honesty is key to realizing that potential.

Tell the truth; face the truth. To be who you are, to live your dreams, will require that you know the truth, and that you handle the truth. Dare to be true to yourself. If you don't dare, then honestly, you don't dare complain.

Don't dare spend all your days deceiving yourself about the people who negatively impact your life. Dare to stop that pattern, now. Don't dare let your life waste away with you in a state of denial. Dare to get real about who you are, what you want, and what you have to do to get where you want to go. Don't dare continue to live in a state of "I wish it were," without reaching into "I will make this happen." Dare to live real. Dare to design your destiny.

None of us need be afraid of our reality. Our true and current conditions are our stepping stones. *Stepping stones are good.* Knowing where to place your foot as you take your next step in life only contributes in a positive way to enabling any of us to move forward. "Getting real" may seem like tough love, or may seem difficult; accepting what we face may even force us out of our comfort zone. But consider this: not knowing where you're going always carries a cost.

None of us need be afraid to get real. Being clear and honest with ourselves about where we are and where we're starting from is the first step. Then, as we move on the way to where we're going, continuing to focus on what's real constitutes a huge and important investment.

Have you turned a deaf ear to someone or something you know you should be listening to? Are you refusing to hear your inner voice? Are you looking at your life with your eyes shut? Are you making a habit of fooling yourself?

Are the teachers always the problem, and your children problem-free? Have you refused to come to terms with the fact that your spouse may be compulsively gambling, or may be putting your family's financial security at risk? Have you noticed your teenager coming home late, with slurred speech or red eyes? Can you just not bring yourself to confront him? Have you convinced yourself that if you confront your teenager, you will alienate yourself as parent?

Dare to face the issues. Dare to take charge.

Today:

Is there a problem in a relationship in your life that you are refusing to acknowledge and deal with honestly? If so, find a quiet time today and reflect upon the circumstances. Resolve before the day is over that you will develop a plan to deal realistically with the issue. Write down specifically how your life will be changed by coming to terms with the situation you have acknowledged.

Dare To...

Look at your life and determine what realities about the people closest to you you need to face.

- Get a grip on your challenges.
- Identify changes that need to be addressed in your relationships in order to live your life on purpose.

Save yourself from living in a state of denial.

- Recognize that nobody's perfect, but also that you don't have to be a victim when someone is hurting you and is unwilling to change.
- Know that being real about your child's problems is good parenting.

Let go of "I wish it were" and concentrate on "I am here, and I can go there."

- Appreciate yourself for who you are.
- Have the greatest expectations for who you can become independent of others.
- Expect yourself to be a problem-solver for the rest of your life.

Nine

Be True to Yourself

Every human being wrestles with the truth, which is why truth has been written about for centuries. Even with all the doctrine to direct us, people still struggle with acknowledging what's real. I have lied to myself in my life, and I have learned that self-deception does not pay.

When we are conscientious and diligent and devoted to making all we can of our lives, we are like sculptors. We all have the power of artists to make what we will of the life we've been given. We can lay our hands on our goals, follow our interests, adjust our habits. We can shape our time and advise our children and effectively manage our future. When we treat our lives with the dedication that living a good life requires, our realities will not turn sour. Our future will respond to our shaping and control.

Being productive and authentic in life requires, first and foremost, that we face the truth. Confucius, one of the world's most famous philosophers, whose words have been repeated for twenty-five centuries, wrote, "The object of the *superior* man is truth." Here the philosopher reflects on the difference between the ordinary person and the person who excels. Truth matters.

Our spirits depend on our honest view of life in order for us to know where we are, and in order for us to determine how to get from there to where we want to go. If we do not know where we are, or if we misread where we are, then the path we take is not likely to lead us to our intended destination.

The great actress and vocalist Pearl Bailey said, "You never find yourself until you face the truth." Facing the truth requires that we make a clear connection between who we are, what we believe, and what we do.

When we think of lying, or of deception, we think most often about lying to others. But in our efforts to get through the hard times in life, we sometimes lie, however gently, to ourselves.

As I covered in the last chapter, when we deceive ourselves about others, we sometimes don't even recognize that we're lying. The stresses of the hour, of the day, or of our lives can compel us to refuse to believe that what we're facing is real. We enter into periods of dishonesty that can be brief or extensive. But we can also lie to ourselves about ourselves—about our own imperfections, our own shortcomings, our own failures. We cannot address what we fail to acknowledge.

When we lie to ourselves, our deception is not always obvious. Instead, self-deception becomes clear to us over time. We don't set out to believe what isn't true. We don't deceive ourselves on purpose. We have other priorities that help us believe the lies we tell ourselves. Though not always intentional or malicious, lying to ourselves can be dangerous. Fortunately, people who love and support us will often speak the truth to us and help shake us out of the dangerous fog of self-deception.

When we deceive ourselves, there is always a cost. Each one of us pays for the time we spend trying to live out a reality that does not match the truth. The price we pay for ignoring the truth increases progressively over time.

If I had to identify a single life philosophy that, for me, rises in importance above all others, I would point to truth-telling. I have seen how destructive dishonesty can be. As I have always said to my children, nothing in life is important enough to lie about.

Let's take our health issues, for example. We hear almost endlessly that obesity is a serious health risk. But many of us choose to believe that we can defy the odds—that obesity statistics don't apply to us. One-third of Americans choose to behave as if we can eat all the junk we want and still survive and thrive. We pretend that twenty pounds overweight won't become forty, won't become sixty, won't kill us. We also decide, through amazing personal deception, that diabetes, high blood pressure, insomnia, joint aches, and back problems associated with being overweight will not befall us because we are different. In fact, we are not different, we are just lying to ourselves.

Similarly, we can recite chapter and verse what the money gurus tell us about the dangers of debt. Yet we continue to spend more than we earn, believing more possessions, a bigger house, or more travel will make us happier. In fact, such tangible signs of the lie can complicate our lives and compound the misery.

Living outside of your truth is not only unhealthy, it's unproductive and depressing. It's only when you are living authentically that you can find and hold on to a place of peace and comfort. Only then can your life be fully open to new possibilities.

I've been there; that's how I know.

What, Me, a Liar?

Although I've always made a heartfelt effort to be truthful, and to hold truth-telling as the standard for myself and for my children, I also have to admit that I have lied to myself. There was a time in my life when I deceived myself and tried to convince myself that my reality was what I wanted to believe, rather than what was true. My own contradiction between the belief I insisted on and the reality I faced even caused me to lie in my dealings with others.

I never lied to myself intentionally. I prided myself on living with my eyes wide open. But at one point in my life, the truth in front of me was so disappointing that I took far, far longer than I should have to accept what was real and to take appropriate action.

For years I didn't fully acknowledge that I was in a marriage that had failed. Not a marriage that might fail, or that might be revived—but a marriage that no longer functioned. The marriage wasn't supporting either one of us, but I did not want to admit that to myself. Even as I reread what I write here, I see remnants of my self-deception. I wrote, "I didn't fully acknowledge" when what I really should have written is, "I pretended." No, not that either. I downright lied to myself!

Years ago, when my marriage was actually crumbling, I did not see the truth, in part because I didn't want to. I wished for a different outcome. I didn't see that I was lying to myself because, I suppose, I felt a little shame about "failing" at marriage.

The thought of letting go of my marriage worried me because of my children. I longed for my two sons to have the kind of beautiful upbringing I had. I and my brothers spent our childhood and youth in a safe, happy household. We had two parents who loved each other deeply, and loved us unconditionally. In our home our parents—who were far from perfect—complemented one another and brought their individual strengths to a successful partnership. The product of their love and effort created a secure, predictable family life for me and my brothers. I knew when I came home every day my family would be intact. We grew up secure and unaffected by any scarcity of attention, love, or affection.

Mom and Dad were hands-on parents who were vigilant in their duties to love and teach us. Their extraordinary partnership made me who I am. Of course, I wanted and planned for the same kind of secure family and devoted upbringing for my children.

But I came to realize that my ex-husband could never be to our children what Dad had been to us, no matter how long I remained in the marriage. I had to find a way to myself provide the love and security I wanted for my children. In time, by identifying what I wanted most for my children, I devoted extra energy to providing them a firm emotional and spiritual foundation. I also worked diligently to be sure they knew that I would listen, and that I would do everything a mother could to support them emotionally.

I had to acknowledge that our future as a family would be differently expressed from what I had known. I had to face that reality.

Don't get me wrong. I continued to worry. I worried about how disrupting our family unit would make me and my sons feel and behave. I worried about how our future outlook would change for me and my children. I worried about whether I could provide for them materially, financially, and even educationally on my own. But the issue of the truth matters here as well. The mental stress and emotional struggle that I would remove from my life was no small matter. A parent at peace is a better parent.

For years, the folks who loved me could see, long before I was willing or able to, that I was walking a dead-end road. I kept "affirming" that my marriage was good, and hoping that the problems between us would disappear. Finally, a good friend of mine shook me out of my fog. "Glenda," he said, "wishing does not make it so. Self-talk is important, but just telling yourself that you want a satisfying, productive marriage won't make your marriage right."

His words that day really touched my heart. He pierced through my self-deception. He basically was telling me, *Girl, you need to get a grip.* What he said to me about my wishful thinking helped me shake off my cloudy confusion and confront the truth that I was already living.

Motivated to look clearly at my situation, I saw that I had been lying to myself about my marriage for years. Good people can be in bad marriages. I had been trying to hold on to the belief that our marriage could be fixed. Actually, I wanted to believe, more specifically, that I could fix it. Not only was I lying to myself about the state of the marriage, but also about wanting to fix it. I had created a lie within a lie. Even while I kept telling myself I wanted the marriage, I was not telling myself the truth.

I went through a period where I repeatedly asked myself sad but critical questions. *Will I stay married? Can our marriage be repaired? Will our children be worse off or better off?* But once the confusion lifted, and because I faced the truth, the difficulty of getting through each day lessened considerably. That drag-yourself-out-of-bed dread I had been living with disappeared. At one point, my anxiety had been so bad that my morning prayer became, "God, let me just get through the day."

I want to take a minute to clarify, though: the decision to divorce did *not* bring me giddy pleasure. I'm too smart and, I hope, too good a mother to be so cavalier. Ending our marriage was a difficult choice that I never took lightly. But once I made the choice, I did feel so, so much better. I'm convinced that I became a better mother and a more productive person once I faced what had to be done.

Part of facing my truth was realizing the importance of peace over position. Choosing to leave my marriage set the ultimate trade-off in motion: I gave up something that might be socially desirable or look good from the outside—my marriage—for something that felt so much better on the inside—a sense of peace.

I'm sure whatever your life experiences have been, you can appreciate the feeling of peace that comes from doing what you know you have to do, instead of trying to avoid the truth.

I had to revisit and reconsider some of my dreams after I divorced my husband. With one month's paycheck in my hand, I left my dream house and nightmare of a marriage. With my husband, we had settled in one of Atlanta's loveliest neighborhoods—an area of spacious brick and stone homes, graceful lawns, and good schools. The boys and I drove out of that beautiful neighborhood, carrying the bare minimum of clothes and other possessions. My emotions were jumbled. I swallowed my pride and headed to my parents' home, where we stayed temporarily with my mother. (My dad had died about nine months before.) I traded the big house and all the trappings for peace of mind and peace in my surroundings. This decision felt as true and authentic as any I'd ever made. Despite the difficulties, I felt centered and at peace. I was so grateful to have the boys and their needs to concentrate on; they focused my efforts and my attentions. Their needs fueled my determination. I grew confident that I would be able to face our immediate and distant future. I gained confidence by focusing on steady progress, and by expressing gratitude for my peace and freedom—moving toward my goals one effort at a time.

After about a year, we moved out to a small but serene place of our own. I traded my dream house for a home full of dreams; I entered a new space where hope could take root and a new phase could begin for our family of three. Our new home, though simpler and smaller, became the place where our hopes and dreams were nurtured into reality. For me, our modest home was a bridge back to wholeness, a place of peace, liberation, and healing. Before long it became a gathering place for all of my sons' friends. We quickly came to feel comfortable and happy there.

By facing the truth, I crossed the bridge to peace and freedom.

Inner Secrets

Taking a long hard look at our inner secrets is well worth the effort. Only we can discern for ourselves whether what we believe and what we say is true. The "big lie" (or lies) we tell ourselves will drain our spirit unless we take action.

We don't feel any better for creating or nurturing or adhering to dishonesty within our own souls. Walking around thinking, *Nobody knows but me*, does not help us gain strength or heal. Furthermore, most of the time this idea is not true. The secrets we carry show in some way—on our faces, in our nervous reactions, in the way we isolate ourselves, in our job performance, in how we relate to family. We lie to ourselves because of what we don't think we can face up to.

Deceiving ourselves is like having a closet full of clothes that don't fit. Not only is our closet cluttered with things we can't use, clothes we won't reach for, clothes we couldn't wear, but we've rendered a valuable space in our lives virtually useless to us. Our spirits are designed to run smoothly on the truth. Our souls are made to help us be who we are. Having a space in our souls cluttered with a lack of authenticity chokes off our chances to thrive and be whole.

There are lots of lies we tell ourselves. We pretend we are content at work when in fact stress, abuse, and overwork are killing us. Many of us profess to love our jobs when what we really love is the prestige, the title, or the privileges. The inner truth, the one we've been unable to face, is that our work does not satisfy us. This kind of deception is critical—and it affects so many of us—because we spend so many of our waking hours working, getting to and from work, and preparing for work. The work we choose to do, or do without choosing to, consumes a huge chunk of our adult lives. But many of us choose to believe that the work we do is not really up to us. The notion of leaving the jobs we have so overwhelms us that we remain in a very negative environment at great cost to ourselves.

We don't tell ourselves the truth—*This job is killing my spirit.* We just go on deceiving ourselves, insisting that we are on the right path, even if we are standing on the wrong side of the street.

We also lie to ourselves about our relationships with substances. Or we deceive ourselves about our emotional patterns. Perhaps you've hidden or deceived yourself about addiction, calling yourself "just a social drinker," even though you've been drinking heavily for decades. Maybe you've convinced yourself that a nightly indulgence in marijuana "helps you relax" when in fact you are unable to function without it. You might be resisting the idea that you are functionally or clinically depressed, yet unable to muster the courage to acknowledge it and seek help.

Holding on to such lies is not necessarily immoral or malicious. We think, at first, that we're protecting ourselves. To admit that we're addicted or dependent on unhealthy behavior is not easy. Often we're just too scared, too low-energy, or too stuck to imagine that we can chart a better course.

Yet...harboring internal lies *can* kill the spirit. Our spirits stay with us, steadily and unfailingly, all of our lives. Our spirits need us to be who God made us to be. Our souls need us to live as who we are—made in the divine image, by a divine hand. Our spirits expect us to stand up and be who we are. Our spirits wilt when we fail ourselves.

There are plenty of people who have managed to cure themselves of denial. Denial is one of the phases of grieving, and all of us grieve:

over the deaths of people and the deaths of things—failed marriages, lost friendships, missed opportunities.

But grief passes. The mistakes we make do get retired to history. If we deny the truth of the mistake, however, we *will* make the same mistake again. If we look at the truth of what we believe, if we take a hard look at how we behave, we stop repeating ourselves. We provide ourselves with the grace and opportunity to change, and to better honor our lives. If we look at ourselves truthfully, we seize the opportunities we are given to show what we are truly made of.

If we don't tell the truth, then we run the risk of forgetting the lie we've told. If we don't tell the truth, then we run the risk of forgetting the person we are. Similarly, if we don't *face* the truth, then we run the risk of never fully living the life we've been granted. Without the truth, we live and die the "easy way," and I guarantee the easy way does not bring fulfillment.

Who Are You Kidding?

May I challenge you to try being true to yourself? To list the ways you feel out of sync, inauthentic, to define how you're "rubbing yourself the wrong way." The key part of this challenge, of course, is to *do something about the disconnect.* Give yourself the gift of your own dedication. Live the life that's true to you.

Is there a lie you're holding on to? Is there something you're ready to face? Do you suspect that you are deceiving yourself and you're just starting to move, however slowly, toward acknowledging the truth? Are you realizing you've got some soul-searching to do, but are hesitating because the truth could be difficult, painful, or humiliating?

First, I applaud you. You deserve encouragement for considering the possibility of facing the lie. Go ahead. Refuse to deceive yourself any longer. By looking the truth in the face, you will be refusing to deceive the person you should treat with the highest respect—*yourself!*

When we tell ourselves the truth, we honor the person to whom we owe the most honesty and the highest morals. When we live our lives honestly, we align ourselves with the divine in us.

Whatever areas in our lives are clouded over by lying, we owe ourselves the warmth and sunshine of the truth. Whether you've lied to yourself about a bad marriage, a health problem, abuse, a financial reality; whether you've deceived yourself about what you're trying to do, or what you're not trying to do—meet the truth head-on. I promise you what you will gain is worth the temporary pain.

Getting to the work you need to do to correct your life is impossible if you refuse to see your life clearly.

By facing the truth we give ourselves strength and help create energy for the challenges, struggles, and victories ahead. Ultimately, we will feel better and we will live better—maybe not immediately, but certainly over time.

Have You Had Enough?

Self-deception lives inside the ultimate private place—inside our minds and our hearts. When we lie to ourselves, we bury the truth. Then we have to take on another task later, digging up and dusting off the truth in order to set ourselves free. Denying the truth *will* block our blessings. Failing to see what's real *will* clutter our souls. Once I admitted that my marriage was over and was unfixable, I opened the door for my life to change radically for the better.

The good news is, accepting the truth we haven't been able to tell ourselves creates defining opportunities in our lives. The truth *will* set you free.

Dare to be who you are. Dare to tell yourself the truth. Whenever you feel the need to, dare to ask yourself the question, *Who am I kidding?*

The truth is that lying to ourselves is not something any of us can do with ease. When we fail to tell ourselves the truth, we do so much damage to ourselves that we often feel the effects in a physical way. For me, my stomach starts to bother me. I feel inauthenticity in my gut, and I have learned to be happy for that signal. It keeps me honest; it keeps me beholden to myself. Do you feel your self-deception physically? Welcome that feeling, and most importantly, respond to that feeling.

There's another expression that people don't use so much anymore—"You're pulling my leg." This idea could use a little dusting off, I think. Because lying and self-deception, however benign, gets us really off balance, just like you would be if someone literally pulled your leg.

Dare to use the strength God gave you. Dare to stand on your own two feet. Each one of us is uniquely equipped to make the best of our own lives. Each one of us is born with the tools to see clearly and live strong.

How dare we deceive ourselves into living a life that is less than the life we could have? How dare we burden our children with a lack of discipline and self-awareness? How dare we destroy our potential with dishonesty?

I say, we don't dare. What do you say? Have *you* had enough?

Have you known for months that you will not be promoted but yet you refuse to develop a plan to either seek a transfer or find a job outside the company? Are you still convincing yourself that you are a social drinker when in fact you are an alcoholic? Have you been engaged for five years already, and yet you still believe that the commitment to marriage is there?

Are you delaying making decisions you know you need to make? What are you refusing to face? How is it affecting your life and the people and relationships in your life?

Today:

Ask this question: *Is there something I am lying to myself about, and why am I refusing to know the truth?* Take time now to write down the lie and explain why you have been lying to yourself. Then write down the truth and explain how you expect the truth to change your life.

Dare To...

Recognize the power in the truth.

- Be honest with yourself, realizing this is a form of self-love.
- Set yourself free by not trapping your life in lies.

Be authentic.

- Let the sunlight of truth help you grow and develop good plans.
- Embrace how liberating living by truth can be.

Live truth to power.

- Abstain from accepting lies and half-truths from others.
- Capture the power to live life fully by being true to your spirit.

Ten

Guilt Can Paralyze You

Our intentions register in our hearts and minds as plans. We go along in our lives, intending to do things, and when we don't act on our plans, we feel guilty. Unless we follow through on our intentions with action, unless we do what we plan, guilt will show up. Sometimes we don't recognize guilt or the source; we just call it stress—the things we meant to do that we didn't get done, yet that continue to hang over us. Guilt arises from a lack of follow-through, and once we feel guilty, we are even less likely to take action. But inaction actually *produces* guilt. After guilty feelings take root, they will keep growing until you face up to them and get rid of those feelings in the garden of your life.

There are two cures for guilt: taking action so that you don't carry guilty feelings around, and forgiving yourself for actions you haven't taken up to now.

Recognizing and Predicting Guilty Feelings

Most of the time, when we don't take action, we have our reasons. We're busy at work. The children. The overtime. The car in the shop. Limited funds. We "plan" to get to whatever we are trying to get to—next week, next month, next time we're in the area, next payday. But sometimes, before we get around to doing what we plan, the time to act has passed. Sometimes the reason we wanted to act has disappeared.

If we learn to recognize when we start feeling guilty, we have done ourselves a great favor. We can use the guilty feeling to trigger us to examine what we're doing or not doing. We can use guilt to warn us to stop and consider what action we need to take. If we don't stop and think when we start to feel guilty, then guilt will rob us of joy we could be seeking, and lock us out of happiness we could be feeling.

Discovering when and why you feel guilty is a step you can take that matters greatly. Knowing what makes you feel guilty can help you stop, reconsider, and do what you intend—rather than doing the usual by putting your good intentions aside. Examine how you might fill in the blanks below.

I feel guilty when:
- I feel like I should _____, but I don't.
- When I intend to _____, but I don't.
- I want to try _____, and I haven't yet.
- I want to do better with _____, but I'm still doing what I've always done.
- I want to do something about _____.
- I want do something for _____, but I haven't seen her/him lately.

Did you fill in all the blanks? Are you tapping into feelings of guilt as you read this? Does something you didn't do, or wish you had done, come immediately to mind?

Use a pencil or a pen. Discover what makes you feel guilty. If you haven't done so already, take the time to finish those sentences. Your answers will create a positive agenda for you to address, as a result of examining what's holding you up.

Guilt Signals Importance

We don't feel guilty about unimportant issues. If we feel guilty, we are neglecting one of our *spiritual priorities*. That's what feeling guilty is teaching us: whatever it is we're avoiding or delaying is important to the person we are.

We must pay attention when we feel guilty, because none of us should allow our spiritual priorities to take a backseat to the immediate demands of life. This is one of the major life lessons we all must face: priorities are bigger than the demands we face daily. Accomplishing our goals will take the accumulated actions of many days, and sometimes years, of our lives. In order to address and reach our dreams, we must take the long view.

Guilt and Inaction Are Two Strands of One Rope

As I mentioned, I had a hard time facing the hard truth about my marriage. I needed to leave. I faced a number of problems, the marriage wasn't working, and I could not fix it by myself. As time passed, I came to know this more and more. And yet I did not act.

I began to feel guilty because I wasn't taking action. Looking back, I can see that guilt took over for my inaction, and guilt kept me in my marriage much longer than I should have stayed. *Guilt began to contribute to my problems.* Because I know how crippling guilt can be, I responded by forging ahead, by taking the hard steps I knew I needed to take. I refused to let my worry or my guilt disrupt my progress. I carried them with me out of the marriage.

Leaving a marriage is of course a huge decision, not one to be made quickly or taken lightly. For a decision as big as divorce, we have to think, go slow, and weigh our situation. No one should rush into divorce, and I am not encouraging that at all. And I do not blame myself for needing to take the time to *be sure* that this was the best decision for me and for my sons. However, of the many lessons I learned or was reminded of as I began to reshape my life, a major one was that I could observe how guilty I felt and understand that, somewhere, I wasn't taking the action that my soul was urging me to take.

I believe in the institution and sanctity of marriage. For children to grow up in a loving, two-parent home was what I thought was ideal. I applaud strong marriages and I wanted one of my own. But I am also a realist. I know that sometimes the only path to family and personal harmony is to eliminate the discord that negatively affects everyone.

Telling our children that we are getting divorced is a sad experience many of us face. It's a heartbreaking moment, even when we know there is no hope for the marriage and feel strongly that we're doing the right thing. I recall this teeter-totter time in my life. From day to day I would conclude, *I simply must do this. I must leave this marriage. It will be better for all of us.* Then five minutes later I'd leap to the opposite conclusion: *There is simply no way I can put these children through a divorce!*

Moving on is not easy, but moving on is necessary. Just because something is not easy does not mean, of course, that we have license to avoid it. Avoidance is hesitation, avoidance is inaction.

But once I knew that my marriage had failed, I couldn't leave—not immediately. I worried: I did not want my children to grow up in a "broken home." I was not ready to give up my plan and my fantasy about my two children and their two parents. I wanted my marriage, or shall I say, I wanted what a marriage represented. I wanted the husband, the stability, the two kids. I basically wanted the symbolism of the marriage, which is what I had. But symbolism is not enough.

I finally had to force myself to accept the truth. The marriage I had wasn't serving me or the children. The marriage I had was broken. The marriage I had did not relate at all to the fantasy I claimed I didn't want to give up.

You can't give up something you don't have. I did not have the marriage I wished for, and I could not make my marriage what I wanted. Not by myself. While I worried, struggled, tried to decide, a dear friend saw my anxiety and preoccupation. "Glenda, I'm really worried about you. You look frail and depleted. I don't even recognize the person in that body anymore." Once I had made the decision and some time had passed, someone else said, "Girl, you look like you've been attached to helium balloons. You've been lifted to a higher place. You seem happy and peaceful for the first time in ages!"

As I saw that my boys were thriving, and that I had made the right choice for our family, the guilt lifted. I took action, and it was difficult, but ultimately it was best. My sons witnessed and I now believe deeply appreciate my work and sacrifices to provide a loving home for them. We did not have the same family we would have had, had I not divorced. But we were able to make a family where there was peace and joy. This transition was not without its challenges, but we managed to make a new family—a different family, where harmony was possible. We pulled together, and we sculpted a new version of family. We worked with each other, toward goals we all knew.

Of course, I know now that there was nothing else for me to do but release myself from my marriage fantasy and start again. I did that, and I survived. I also thrived. All three of us thrived. I had been at a very low point in my life, but I needed to make a change. I was trying to survive in a bad marriage, and when I moved myself out, I got on a new track that was inaccessible to me while I kept myself trapped. If I had not taken action, my guilt would have been worse, for sure, and much longer-lasting. None of us ever knows exactly where a different road would have taken us. But I can say one thing for sure: if I had stayed for reasons of guilt and worry, I certainly would not be where I am today.

Yes, I felt guilty—perhaps disappointed is a better word—that my sons would not have a traditional family. But things at home weren't going to get better. Feeling confident that I was making the right choice helped me move forward, and helped relieve the guilt.

Cure #1: Take Action

If there *is* something we can do to correct the current causes of our guilty feelings, then—oh, happy day. We can get to it. We can make up for our past lapses *by taking action*.

- We can follow through on our intentions.
- We can act on our plans.
- We can do what we need to do, now.

Guilt cannot survive where action rules. Taking action is the solution, especially when you compare the feeling of guilt with the amazing feeling of ease and productivity that comes with working on the projects and the issues you intend to. Our spirits are what make us unique, and our spirits are always encouraging us to become who we are destined to become. As long as we are attending to our motivations, our talents, and our heartfelt desires, we won't need to feel guilty. Taking action works to keep our lives in motion; inaction makes our spirits feel that we are uncommitted to who we are and to what we are divinely driven to do in this life.

We can all ask ourselves when we feel guilty, *What am I not doing?* The cure will be to renew and speed up our efforts to do what we're avoiding or delaying. Or we can decide we are not going to do that, let go of the guilt, and move on. Making this decision is taking action too.

There is a longtime friend of our family whom we call Mother Cloud. I have known Mother Cloud forever, and I knew her husband too, before he passed. They were married sixty years. After Mother Cloud became a widow, I intended to look in on her more often. They had no children. I loved Mother Cloud and her fine husband. I enjoyed seeing them and spending time with them every time we got together. As a widow, after sixty years of devoted marriage, it was an adjustment for Mother Cloud. She needed reaching for, and I intended to reach for her, to fold her more closely into our family and ensure she remained all right.

Did I? Not at first. I intended to, and I thought about it, but then I got busy, and I didn't reach out. (Perhaps you can see a pattern in the intentions I fail to attend to? My spirit wants me to be a connected person, a person who showers others with "family love." But my life distracts me. This is a lesson I've learned.) I intended to call Mother Cloud, but then there was the plane to catch, and there was the show to tape, and there were my sons and their events, and all I had to do. And then, mercifully, a Mother's Day came.

I called Mother Cloud for Mother's Day and asked her to come to brunch with us. She agreed. I was grateful when she joined our family for brunch, and she was glad to be invited and to be remembered. Like

I said, Mother Cloud has been part of our extended family, so her presence at Mother's Day was easy and made perfect sense.

Divine timing. At that brunch, I asked Mother Cloud to join us for Mother's Day brunch, and for our family Christmas brunch—every year forward. Now, thanks to that one action—making that one Mother's Day call—we have a date with Mother Cloud twice a year. I no longer have to worry about whether I am "getting to" Mother Cloud. I have handled the need I have to check in on her. I don't have to feel guilty. Neither May nor December will pass by without my "remembering" that Mother Cloud should be there, should be called, should be picked up, should be checked in on. It only took one phone call, and now Mother Cloud has family times, with our family. I make it a point to call her from time to time to just chat. Reaching out does not have to be overly complicated. Connections can be easy to maintain, and quite honestly, our humanity depends on our connections. Maintaining relationships with others demands that we take action. The action we take does not have to be grand or large. *The action we take just has to be taken.*

This is how guilt can be avoided: if we remember to take action, if we respect our intentions, if we do something when thoughts cross our mind.

Because guilt comes and takes hold of us when we are not doing what we know we need to do, it is often partnered with other feelings of sadness and disappointment. Guilt is a feeling that should provoke us to action. Guilt should cause each one of us to go swiftly forward and do exactly what we need to do.

Cure #2: Forgiveness

For many of us, forgiving ourselves is difficult. It may even be an experience we have never had. So many of us look to others for approval. If we are one of those folks—people whose interactions with their own hearts and spirits are limited—then the idea of being in charge of our own forgiveness may seem new, and may also seem too hard to do. Even so, forgiving ourselves is necessary. Forgiving ourselves is the ticket to moving into a new place. Forgiving ourselves will untangle us from immobility.

We have to practice being forgiving. We have to forgive ourselves for things we haven't done so far, and that we won't get done because we can't do what we planned or wanted anymore. The person is gone, the time is gone, the need is gone.

In the instances where the situation can no longer be corrected, the first step we have to take is to forgive ourselves for what we cannot currently change. Forgiveness allows us to take future action with greater speed, with seriousness, and with respect for the good we intend to do. Forgiveness permits us to let go of our guilt and to focus, with determination, or to take actions that make sense now, and avoid any future guilt about the same issues.

When we let guilt distract or delay us, we do serious damage. By entertaining guilt and inaction in our lives, we kill our goals and ambitions, we silence our hopes and dreams. In order to accomplish what we want to accomplish, in order to live out the agendas our spirits set for us, we have to let go of guilt and go forward, performing to the best of our abilities, doing the challenging work that our lives present. We have to practice forgiving ourselves for what we have not done so far, so that the grace to do what we need to go forward can expand and support our priorities.

Loving your family, your children, and wanting to give them the best can make you feel guilty about all kinds of choices you know you need to make. I think all working parents share the challenge of balancing jobs and parenthood. Guilt over our families can also keep us from doing what we know it's time to do.

When I started my new job at Delta Air Lines, my son was six months old. After I hugged and kissed him, and checked for the umpteenth time that everything was in order, I walked out of the front door of our home to my brand-new high-powered job in the legal department. I was excited about blending motherhood and a challenging new position.

Two steps toward the driveway it hit me. I was leaving a helpless, precious child who desperately needed me. What in the world was I thinking? How could I possibly even consider doing this? Sure, I had spent nearly every minute of his first half-year of life with my baby. And I had hired Mrs. Howard, a lovely and experienced woman, to care for him.

I stopped, sat down on my front step, and just started wailing. Head in my hands, I bawled like a baby. The sound, which I tried to muffle, of course attracted the attention of Mrs. Howard. I remember this like it was yesterday.

Bless her heart, Mrs. Howard sat right down next to me, looped her arm around my heaving shoulders, and could not have been sweeter. I was worried that she would think I didn't trust her. But wise Mrs. Howard knew that that wasn't it at all.

"Now, what seems to be the problem?" she asked me.

"Oh, I don't exactly know, Mrs. Howard," I stuttered through my sobs. "I was fine five minutes ago. You saw. But as soon as I started for the car something just hit me. I feel so . . . guilty!" Just saying the word unleashed another round of tears, and I actually put my head against her shoulder. Mrs. Howard reminded me that there was absolutely no reason to feel guilty. I was certainly not doing anything wrong and, what's more, it takes a lot of energy to feel guilty. "I believe with that big job of yours and this little baby, you're going to need all the energy you can find."

Mrs. Howard was right. I couldn't afford to wallow in a cloud of confusion. My work required a high level of concentration. I needed to focus at work, so that when I got home in the evening, I could focus on the very important work at home—being a mother, and wife, and person in my own right.

Trying to better understand what I was feeling helped relieve the guilt. In my case, the guilt was largely based on fear that I would miss something. His first word . . . the first time he tossed a toy from his high chair . . . the first time he clutched a crayon. The classic first step.

But I concluded that what I really needed to focus on was being the kind of mother who could help him plan his future steps through life—to help order his steps into manhood. And for me that included being a productive professional. I needed the balance of a professional career.

Once released from the chokehold of my guilt, I truly loved both parts of my life. It wasn't easy, but no one ever said it would be. I was a corporate lawyer, and I still spent my fair share of nights in the emergency room with a child's asthma attacks, high fevers, and one of those frightening falls kids take. I was also a mom catching lots of early-bird flights to try cases in courtrooms across the country.

Yes, I was a corporate attorney flying around the country. But I'm no different from a dad who works the third shift and can't be around to help with homework . . . or a firefighter who's called in at any hour . . . or the military mom serving our country from thousands of miles away.

It's the same for the single factory worker who's forced to leave his kids with a neighbor who, he worries guiltily, may not be the best influence, but is the only choice he's got. Resources do not necessarily solve the problem of parental guilt. Guilt knows no socioeconomic or gender boundaries. We all struggle with this problem.

For me there is no question that working has made me a better mother. Most days, my life felt balanced and productive on both fronts. Later, my children told me that they feel more broadly educated, and that they feel like they've had richer experiences, with me working while they were growing up. I modeled behavior that aimed for success, and now my sons are on the path.

Many parents add yet another layer of guilt by feeling that because they are away from their kids while at work, they don't "deserve" any time to themselves. Some parents forgo exercise, self-care, or even spiritual development because they don't want to sacrifice more time away from the kids. We have to take care of ourselves. If we don't, then we cannot be there for the children, we cannot be all we need to be for them.

The smart choice is striking a balance. Doing what we need to do to be productive, healthy, and well-adjusted can help us be better, more patient parents. I have not always been good at striking the balance that I know is so important. I have to confess that I still struggle to take care of myself, with all the other things I have going on. Striking a balance is still a challenge for me. But I continue to try to create the space I need to make myself a priority, at least some of the time.

In time, I acknowledged that I needed the balance of being a mom *and* a professional woman, and that doing so with as little guilt as possible was the only way it was going to work.

Remember the Lesson

When we let go of guilt, we have to *remember the lesson.* If we learn the lesson, then there's been a payoff for the time we spent feeling guilty. The payoff is not, of course, as beneficial as stepping up to our intentions in the first place. What we intended was to honor our friendships, or to be present for our children, or to show our affection to a relative. But since we were not able to make (*you name what belongs here*) happen, we have to let go of the guilt we feel for what we didn't do. We have to move forward, having learned, and make sure we do what we can, now and in the future, being mindful of the change we need to make. Not only do we have to make the change. We also must live the lesson.

Is there something you feel tremendously guilty about right now? Have you missed an opportunity at work that you should have tenaciously pursued? Are you remembering a love relationship that ended badly? Did you have a sick relative whom you meant to visit, but didn't before they passed away? Have you engaged in malicious gossip? Have you told a lie you that you knew would really hurt the other person? Are you still thinking about a time you turned your back on someone in need? Have you forgiven everyone who has asked? Have you been living with the guilt of being a working parent and not spending enough time with your children or your aging parents?

What guilt do you feel, and how can you move beyond it? Maybe you should write a letter of apology. Maybe you have to actually look the person in the eye and sincerely say you are sorry. Maybe you can make up for an omission. Perhaps in the case of working-parent guilt, you simply have to say to yourself, *I am doing the best I can*. And then you ought to forgive yourself.

Guilt can rob you of your joy. We are meant to live a joyful life. Our days should be full of hope and possibilities. Dare to take charge: deal with whatever guilt you may be carrying today. Discover, act, forgive.

Today:

Scan your heart and spirit for guilty feelings. Decide today where those feelings are coming from. Write down what you discover. Decide what you need to do to resolve the guilt. Decide today. Perhaps you need to ask for forgiveness, or perhaps you need to forgive yourself. Experience the joy of liberating yourself, so you can move on.

Dare To ...

Avoid the way guilt can rise up, seize you, and slow down your progress.

- Start to notice what makes you feel guilty and when.
- Be attentive to your triggers, and make new choices.
- Make your progress your priority.

Resist the gap between your intentions and what you actually do.

- Take action.
- Stop overplanning: be realistic about what you want to accomplish.
- Review your plans frequently and set priorities.

Forgive yourself for what you haven't done.

- Invest in your spiritual health by letting go of guilt when there's nothing you can do.
- Keep moving.
- Do not allow guilt paralysis to consume the days of your life.

Eleven

Your Past Does Not Define Your Future

Everyone gets pushed to the brink at some point in their lives. If you're leading a risky life, getting pushed to *your* brink can be more dangerous than for others who may have more of a safety net. The cushion in life, the safety net, comes from not living on the edge. If you live life on the edge, then stumbling or falling down can often mean falling off a precipice, or falling off a bridge into whatever waters run below.

Life does not promise ease. Most people do get knocked around by the trials we face. Langston Hughes wrote about this so poetically many years ago, when he wrote his famous line, "Life for me ain't been no crystal stair."

You could say life is hardly a crystal stair for most of us. Even the most successful people struggle. The key is to struggle for an outcome that benefits you. Battling for success within a context of destructive options—like being a gang kingpin, like stealing without getting caught,

135

like getting away with what your parents forbid, like getting paid for work you didn't do—only contributes to further destruction. If you let destructive behaviors overtake you, life can destroy you. We are what we choose to do.

Every day we live and every choice we make represents an opportunity to modify who we are. If we change our choices, then we change who we are. It is impossible to do good and not be good. It is impossible to be generous and not be a kind person. It is impossible to work diligently to use your God-given mind and not be a thinker and a thoughtful person in the world.

It's important, most important, to approach life choices knowing this truth—if you have new thoughts, if you make new choices, you can change your life. Your past does not have to define your future. Your future defines your future. The choices you make going forward are the actions that define who you are. This may seem obvious to some people, but to those who have repeatedly messed up, or been messed with, the opportunities of the future are not always so apparent. Consider the choices you will make from today forward, from this moment forward, to be like the alluring warmth of sunshine. Make strong, positive choices, learn from mistakes you've made before, and then leave the burden of your past behind.

Beyond Childhood

Candace was a beautiful teenager who came before me in court. If you didn't know better, if you weren't aware of why a young person would show up in my courtroom, you could easily have mistaken her for a cheerleader or a student council president. When Candace stood before me in court, I saw a familiar sight: an able and physically healthy teenager, unable to cope and acting out. Her eyes were deeply troubled. She either did not know or did not care to make eye contact. Traumatized and overdramatized teenagers will often avoid eye contact, which does not work in their favor. Sometimes teenagers will also try to "stare you down." This too is problematic, and disrespectful.

Candace's behavior swung from one extreme to the other. She would not look at me directly part of the time, but when pushed, she became angry and belligerent and glared at me as if she thought she could stare me down.

Although I don't think she was aware, Candace wore her pain openly on her face and in her body language. Most teenagers do not realize that they are still children, or that they are still quite young, and that I can see through their posturing.

Candace showed drastic differences in her behavior. One minute she seemed deeply depressed, and almost the next minute she could seem very defiant, as if one part of her felt trapped and regretful, and another part was deceitful and out of bounds. For a child of fifteen, this girl was totally out of control. Her behavior was destructive for herself and for others.

Her mother reported that Candace had tried to commit suicide—not once but twice—heavy-duty counseling was part of the "prescription" for Candace. Suicide attempts are nothing you can ignore. Candace's second suicide attempt led her sad and angry mom to reach out to me through my show, hoping that one of our "reality check" interventions could save her daughter. Candace did seem to need saving—from herself.

In the courtroom, Candace seemed hollow. At first I wondered whether her mother had exaggerated about how she behaved. Candace just did not initially strike me as the kind of child her mother described. The social worker on staff had interviewed both the mother and the child. But the more I talked to Candace, the more I began to suspect that she *was* the kind of child her mother and the social worker were describing.

As always, I asked many questions. I try to get a good sense of what a teenager knows about life, what they understand about the requirements of daily living, about how they participate in life and where they are in the process of growing up. In answering my questions, she informed me that she was working as a stripper, that men paid her $300 to peel off her clothing for their lurid enjoyment. I did not believe her for a minute.

I explained to her that I'd been a judge for a long time. I gave her a chance to tell the truth. "Candace," I asked, "do you expect me to believe people pay you $300 just to take your clothes off? Candace, have you been prostituting yourself?"

She answered, "No, Judge, no way, no ma'am, absolutely not."

Her reply did not seem at all true. I felt that she had invented the stripping story.

Drilling down to the real facts of a case—what exists beyond the documents—that's my job, my duty as a judge. I did not hesitate to confront Candace. This case, like others, proved I'm good at uncovering the truth.

Suspecting that Candace might have been prostituting herself, I decided to give her what her mother had come for: a reality check. As a teenager, she clearly needed a jolt to help her understand that what she was doing was a small part of a big world. Young people often don't realize the extent of the many illegal systems and networks that can ensnare them. Most teenagers have not learned enough about life, or about crime and criminals, to realize that what seems small, personal, or harmless to them is actually tremendously different than that. I see young people walking through a gate—at the beginning of a long and ugly road. Most teenagers don't hear the gate click shut behind them. They believe they know better whether they are safe or not than the adults who love them. Many teenagers, because of their age and because they are on the precipice of adulthood, don't see the risks they take as leading to real consequences. They are accustomed to the minor punishments of childhood; they expect that they will be able to recover from anything they do. The truth is, however, that teenagers can cause adult-size problems; teenagers can make long-term mistakes. Teenagers can lock themselves away from basic opportunities by ignoring the advice of their elders and people who love them.

Candace convinced herself that we could not see through her story. And like many teenagers, she didn't perceive that what she was doing was "all that bad." Candace's behavior was already serving her very poorly, she was losing her mother's patience, and she was putting herself at risk. Further, she seemed to ignore that her actions could have potentially tragic results. Any adult can tell you that a fifteen-year-old attempting to hold her own on the streets was not safe.

The interventions I design in situations like this are usually dramatic, and are sometimes painful. I've sent drug dealers to hospital neonatal units, to watch crack-addicted babies suffer. I staged a funeral to show an alcoholic father that he was drinking himself into an early grave. I sent a dangerous teen who boasted that he was unafraid of death to the morgue, where the coroner pulled back the sheet on a young body riddled with bullets.

My goal is always the same—to turn on a shower of reality so cold and shocking that it cuts through deceit and self-deception. I try to create interventions that can permanently change behavior.

I believe in interventions of *experience*. Most people, especially young people, learn through experience and not through speech. The interventions I design are all about *waking people up*.

For Candace, I came up with a very direct plan that involved one-on-one time with a former hooker named Pommie. I arranged for the two of them to spend a night streetwalking. This plan was a bit risky and would likely send Candace for a visit deeper in the world she was flitting around the edges of. I hoped to show her, by sending her out with Pommie, what she had to look forward to if she continued along the path she was currently choosing.

My staff has stopped getting surprised by some of my over-the-top intervention ideas. They were not surprised about what I was sending Candace to experience, although some were a little apprehensive.

They considered how best to protect a fifteen-year-old from the dangers of the streets. They worried that the presence of cameras and crew might anger somebody they'd be wise not to annoy. For the *Judge Hatchett* crew, streetwalking was definitely new territory. But the staff fully embraced the concept, and I love them for their spirit in the name of creating meaningful interventions!

Candace did not want to go. But she was too worn out to protest—as I said, she seemed more or less hollow at this point. Of course, how hollow she felt as a teenager does not compare at all to what she had to look forward to if she did not change her ways.

Remember, Candace had tried not once but twice to commit suicide. She felt she had nothing to live for. But that day, she acknowledged at some level that this intervention was the only thing she had going for her, and agreed to our plan. Although I knew in my heart this idea had great potential, I had concerns about the execution of the intervention, and what impact it would have on this sad young girl.

The Intervention

The night our producers chose for the intervention was warm and dry. Picture the scenario. Pommie leads Candace into one of New York's sketchiest neighborhoods. The camera crew keeps at a distance, following without intruding. Candace and Pommie make their way around the infamous corners where Pommie used to work. I could not have chosen a better "guide." Pommie knew the ropes, or the tricks, I might say. She was also so brutalized by her former work that she had been glad to get out with her life. She could speak the language of the profession that Candace appeared to be just entering. Perhaps the team would be able to see her future, either in the corners they walked or in the older woman who walked with her.

From the tape the crew shot that night, it's easy to see that Candace and Pommie made a connection. At one point, Pommie put her arm around Candace's shoulders. You often see their heads bent close in conversation as they walk. Pommie points to dark alleyways and gestures at poorly lit walk-ups. We perceive that these are places she knows too well.

Pommie told Candace how it felt when men would roll down their car windows, the combination of thrill and shame as she negotiated terms and discussed the details. She showed Candace where she turned her first trick. Where her pimp gave orders and collected money. Pommie reported that men from this building were some of her most dangerous johns. Over there was the favorite strip of a girl who went out on a job one night and never came back. On and on, as they walked, Pommie identified the haunts and the road signs of a complicated and tragic life. Pommie was a woman with battle scars. To hear her tell her story, to have her near you telling her story, was to be with the walking wounded.

We heard about the sad circumstances that led Pommie to the street, her luckless and chaotic life. The saddest and most sobering part of her story was the sense of *inevitability* about choosing this life, about prostitution as a way to live.

After several hours of walking and talking, Pommie led Candace and the cameras down several dark blocks to a bridge over a small stream. There the conversation took a whole new turn.

"Okay, Candace," Pommie said as they leaned over the bridge, staring into the night and the shifting waters below. "Here's where it all went down." Candace turned toward her, trying to make a connection. Clearly something happened here that Pommie had talked about before.

"That's right, Candace," Pommie continued. "This is the exact spot where a john beat me, threw me over the bridge, and left me for dead. Dead."

None of my shows or interventions is ever scripted, so this moment was a shock to us all. The camera captured the women in dim moonlight, their figures and swinging ponytails creating eerily similar silhouettes. The drama of the shot was matched by the drama of the revelation. Although my producers had spent time with Pommie and knew most of her story, they hadn't heard this report before. It's just horrible to imagine, but true.

Now we'd gone beyond the exchange of sex for money. Now we were talking—and Candace was hearing—about hard-core, life-threatening risk. The camera cut from the two women to the murky water. It was impossible not to care.

Taping ended near dawn. The crew was exhausted but thrilled with the footage they'd captured. They believed that this intervention would make a difference; they believed they'd trained the cameras on everything to support making the show. Early the next morning I received a call from the lead producer, who told me things went well. She also reported that Pommie said she needed to see me. I couldn't imagine why we needed to meet, but we hastily arranged a meeting.

For privacy, we met alone in my office at the studio. I had met

Pommie once before, and we exchanged friendly greetings as I invited her to have a seat and offered her coffee.

"Judge, there's something else that happened to me and I want to tell Candace about it." My quizzical silence encouraged Pommie to continue. "I'm HIV-positive," she announced, and this was stunning news to me. Pommie's announcement showed that she had really bought into this reality check. She believed in what we were doing and was totally straight with us. Now she felt compelled to inform Candace about this consequence of her former street life. She wanted to let Candace know during the "back in court" session that concludes an intervention. I wasn't convinced that this was the best decision for Pommie. Nobody in her support network knew this. Anybody who loved or knew her might find out about her condition on television.

"Look, Pommie," I said, "you've been incredibly helpful to us, and I hope to Candace. Your segment will be helpful to others who will be watching. It's evident already that you've put your heart into this. But disclosing that you are HIV-positive on national television? Do you really want to do that?"

She said she did.

In conversation with Pommie, I decided that this was her decision, not mine. But I wanted Pommie to be fully aware of all the implications and possible consequences. So I delayed assembling and airing the show. I arranged for her to see a wonderful counselor, whom we knew would be most appropriate to deal with this issue. Pommie agreed to see the counselor, and she seemed to be relieved to have a space to talk about this. I hoped she would get a realistic idea of what revealing this news could actually mean. The announcement would surely strengthen the impact of our intervention, but it might also hurt Pommie. I should say, might hurt Pommie further, given the devastation of HIV. Of course, there are plenty of people living with HIV, but that does not diminish the initial devastation of learning that your immune system has been compromised by your own behavior, and that your life chances may be greatly diminished.

Several days later, the psychologist assured me she believed Pommie was strong and aware enough to make her own decision. We returned to the courtroom to tape the last segment. Pommie, Candace, and Candace's mom were all on hand. I recapped the situation. We rolled footage of the intervention. The courtroom was very still and quiet as we watched the edited tape of the amazing night on the streets. The drama built as Candace and Pommie hovered at the bridge—there were even a couple of gasps from the audience as Pommie described the beating and being cast into the water. After the tape ended, Pommie turned to Candace, a slight tremble to her voice, but still strong.

"Candace, I guess you have a pretty good idea now about the things that can happen to girls out there. It's so scary and so dangerous. I hope with all my heart that what you've seen will make you change your ways. But there's one more thing that happened to me that you didn't see, because it's invisible. I wanted to tell you that I'm HIV-positive."

Murmurs of "Oh no" echoed through the courtroom. Candace and her mom looked shocked. Even the bailiff was stunned.

Pommie continued to talk. "Candace, I can't change anything I've done. I can't be fifteen again, like you. I can't undo all the destructive decisions that changed my life forever and got me to the place where I've ended up. No way I can do that. But you can. There's still time for you to turn things around in your life. You can have a very different future than mine, if you want to."

The emotional temperature in the courtroom was high. Pommie was teary-eyed. I was doing my best to hold it together from the bench. Believe me, I know better than to mistake a few tears for sincere repentance, but something made me know Candace was serious about change.

Now, fast-forward with me a couple of years. Although it's impossible to stay in touch with all of the thousands of people who pass through my courtroom, I managed to keep in contact with Candace. She was a young, misguided girl when she was in my courtroom. Who wouldn't want to try to save her, at her precious age? I discovered that she has discovered what really lies inside her. She has stopped her destructive behavior and has turned her life around. She has done what I dream of for all the people I work with—she's actually created a whole new life.

Soon after our intervention, she and her mom relocated and started all over in Texas. Candace became an honor student who abstained from sex. She tutored and mentored kids after school. She appears modest and amazing and deeply changed.

We're told that it was those last moments in the courtroom—when Pommie begged her to choose another path—that shook Candace to the core. "If I could only be fifteen again," Pommie had said. Candace had come from a misguided and dangerous place to discover the power in her own choices, and to invest in the future of her choosing. It was a future I could see from where I sat—a gap I wanted desperately to help her cross.

There is an amazing postscript to this story. I ended up sending Candace and Pommie out together on another intervention with a seventeen-year-old, who had had 105 sex partners by the time she ended up in my courtroom. This risky sexual activity was hard to believe, but impossible to ignore. Candace and Pommie were a formidable team. To see them out on the streets again, sharing their strength with another lost and lonely girl, was powerful.

*   *   *

Candace got an education from Pommie and from the intervention. She got an opportunity to look into the future and to learn what her coming days would be like if she continued to make the kinds of choices she had begun to make.

Candace can identify this time, this intervention, as a wide door into her future. She stood at the threshold, which opened to a future where she could change her behavior with new information. She could see that a tragic future was virtually guaranteed if she continued to participate in the scene she had been dabbling in. She could see that her life would most likely spiral down into greater risk and possible disease if she offered her body casually and without adequate concern or care for herself. If she was able to be even a little bit wise, she could see that if she walked through the door of opportunity and carefully considered each choice she was making, she could leave her tawdry past in her history. She could go forward without leaning over a scary bridge. With the new knowledge she had, Candace worked hard and developed a future that is based on greater self-respect.

Candace succumbed to distractions, and the road ahead was *not* easy. But the road could certainly be different, and vastly more positive, than her experience of exploiting herself for the short-term "reward" of $300.

Even with all the mistakes she made, even with the grave disappointments she caused for her family, she still made a positive and productive life for herself. Our choices add up to make our lives. Candace changed her choices.

Most of us can identify at least one time in our lives when we have taken an action that does not support our overall goals. We all have done something, sometime, that goes against how we see ourselves. We have all behaved in ways that do not promote our image or expectations of ourselves. Sometimes, these behaviors are termed self-destructive. And although none of us *wants* to be self-destructive, we all are vulnerable to making choices that do not serve us. In the best circumstances, the damage we do by temporarily forgetting ourselves is minimal and does not cause lasting harm to us or to those who love us.

How many of us have a relative or friend or loved one who we *know* is smarter, more capable, more proficient than they seem to believe? How many of us have friends or coworkers or family members who stay stuck in one place, when we are certain that if they would just take the appropriate steps, they would accomplish what they say they want to do? How many of us know people who think any risk is too much, and so they live their lives doing work that makes them unhappy? How many of us have refused to see our own strength or capability?

The hard truth about not living up to our own possibilities and potential is that we nurture a kind of secret shame. Our shame may be so secret that we can barely acknowledge to ourselves how we feel about ourselves.

Negative Behavior/Positive Behavior

Who we are and what we are meant to do in this life does not change because we refuse to step up to our potential. The geniuses among us remain geniuses, even if we refuse to go to college, even if we refuse to finish high school. The artist within us does not disappear just because we are too worried to pick up a paintbrush or purchase a canvas. Even if we never have a piano, and never learn to sing, the musician born in some of us does not die. If we decide we are going to work in McDonald's, the artist we were born to be puts on that uniform, goes to McDonald's, and quietly—maybe resentfully—checks out the graphic designs that promote McDonald's. The artist would so much rather be doing that art.

When we ignore our instincts, our motivations, and our talents, our souls are not happy. Part of what makes us distressed certainly has to do with the pressures we face in life; feelings of distress or despair, however, also relate to how closely we attend to our motivations and talents. When we fail ourselves by not responding to our motivations and our needs, we open ourselves up to depression, despair, and yes, self-destructive behavior. All of us need our own attention in order to thrive. We need our own commitment to healthy behavior, which includes eating healthier food, getting sufficient exercise, visiting the outdoors in the daylight, laughing every day, communicating with others, and showing and receiving love. We all need to be invested in our physical and emotional and spiritual health. We all need to require that our relationships show respectful and honorable love—both in the way we love others and in the way we receive love from others. We all need to perform productive work.

When we don't invest in our physical, spiritual, and emotional health, then we develop major or minor self-destructive behaviors.

Not all self-destructive behavior seems serious at the outset. Not all self-destructive behavior even seems self-destructive. But whenever we make choices that don't *positively* serve our physical health, our mental health, or the important goals we have for our lives, then we run the risk of becoming self-destructive. Behaviors that do not meet the standard of self-love are behaviors that can become self-destructive. Some people bite their nails. Others occasionally or consistently overeat. Some people drive too fast, running the risk of accident. Some people drink too much or, worse, drink and drive. There are a whole range of nonviolent and violent behaviors that can be classified as self-destructive. In general, if we are not offering ourselves careful and thoughtful self-love, then we are likely on the path of self-destruction. Again, self-destructive behavior can seem minor in the beginning. But violence against others and violence against ourselves can begin with a seemingly minor lack of self-care or self-love. Where negative behavior is involved, however, where we start is often miles away from where we end up. This is true of positive behavior as well, but no one ever complains about moving miles forward in a positive direction. Only when our progress is negative or backward do the miles we travel become a problem.

For me, when young people spend their precious youth engaged in self-destructive patterns, I feel particularly saddened and concerned. The divine order of human life is that we have the most energy to learn and to make rapid progress when young. All the areas of knowledge that some of us take for granted are most appropriately presented and most easily absorbed when the mind is most curious and our energy level is highest. When we fail to learn how to live, when we do not know the spiritual rules that keep us grounded, when we do not learn social rules that make our lives with others possible, then we set ourselves up for self-destruction. Our implosion is only a matter of time.

Carrie, a young woman in her early twenties, came to my courtroom a drug addict and the mother of a young child. Carrie's mother, Mary, brought her to me. Originally from Baltimore, Carrie did not show the expected or stereotypical characteristics of a young white woman raised solidly middle-class. In court, Mary explained with great sadness that Carrie was neglecting her toddler. Carrie's mother was very concerned about her daughter, a striking young redhead who seemed to be giving her life over to crack.

Carrie's failings had an enormous impact on her mother, beyond the devastation of realizing that her daughter was not maturing into a responsible adult. Mary was currently raising Carrie's baby. As is true for many caretaking grandparents, this did not seem to be a situation that she was prepared for. She hoped I could come up with a reality check that would jolt her daughter into awareness and action.

With her family's support, I decided to send Carrie to a thirty-day drug rehabilitation program. This was a traditional response, but rehabilitation has proven effective *for those who want to change.* Plans were set in motion for Carrie, but the morning she was to be driven to the center, she disappeared. No one knew where she had gone. Carrie wasn't just absent for a few hours. She disappeared for four months. Investigators from my show were dispatched to search for her, but they came up empty.

Carrie's sister, Melissa, was desperate to find her. Family bonds do survive these kinds of shocks to the system. We sent Melissa out with our on-staff family advocate to look for Carrie in places that Melissa could think of. Every hot lead turned cold. For a while it seemed like every time our crew got close, Carrie had "just left" some run-down apartment or some seedy bar. Melissa prowled the streets carrying photos of her sister. She was determined not to lose Carrie to a life that excluded her loving family.

Melissa and our family advocate continued to follow any leads, and ultimately they found her. But Carrie was in a tragic state, frighteningly worse off than she had appeared in court several months before. She was discovered lying balled up in the fetal position on a filthy sofa in a crack house. Her condition was a terrible shock to Melissa, in spite of the relief of finding Carrie alive.

Carrie was rail-thin, her red hair knotted and filthy; there were infected track marks up and down her scrawny arms. Imagine the worst images you've seen of crack addicts in the movies or on TV. Now imagine it worse. That's how the family advocate and Melissa found Carrie.

Our advocate, who knew this scenario only too well, got necessarily tough with Carrie and raised her voice to cut through her fog. "Get up, Carrie. We've come to get you out of here. Let's go. Now." Carrie's rescuers half-dragged her away from there, and did not find it easy to manage a steep, narrow flight of steps with Carrie's unresponsive body in tow.

Within a couple of days of her rescue, Carrie was back in my courtroom. Predictably, her eyes filled with tears. She voiced the hollow-sounding promises I've heard so often. *I'm going to change. I want to change. I want to take care of my child. I don't want to keep doing this to my family.*

With Carrie standing before my bench, I said, "Carrie, I cannot force you to go to rehab or make other changes until—or unless—you accept the fact that you're an addict. Until you're prepared to do something about it, there's really nothing I can do. Is it possible for you to start to believe that what you've done in the past does not have to predict what you'll do in the future?

"Yes, you have lied to all of us. You failed to live up to a promise you made to your family and to this court. I'm sure you've failed to keep promises to lots of other people. And more importantly, you failed to live up to the promise you made to yourself and your precious child. But all these things don't have to keep happening. *Your past does not have to define your future.*"

Melissa was in tears. "All I want is my sister back," she cried. "All my mother wants is her daughter back."

As for Carrie, she was spent. Frail, tired, and sick of it all, she agreed to go to rehab. Although at the moment she could not see her way across the great hole that she had dug for herself, the huge gap that divided her past from her future, I could. I have told so many people in my courtroom that I can see beyond the gap, I can see the other side where hope still lives. The ability to envision the possibilities motivated me to work hard for Carrie. I believed this young woman could make it.

I am pleased to report that Carrie found the inner strength to acknowledge and begin to deal with her addiction. She finally woke up from the long night of addiction and the habit of going missing, to deal honestly and directly with her choices. I believe she left there really believing that her past did not have to define her future.

The Past Is No Prison

Sometimes, people we know and love do not seem to love themselves as much as we do, or as much as we think they should. Sometimes, people we know and love don't even seem to *know* themselves. Certainly, when the young people in our families, and the young people we've come to know and love, fail to even understand, much less live up to, their divine potential, those of us looking on feel despair for them. All we want is for young people to realize that (a) they are divinely created, and are destined to live the best life they can, if they are willing to consistently make their best effort, and (b) this is the one life they get, and making the most of the one life they have is work they must do for themselves.

So many parents and relatives and teachers and ministers and mentors that I've met in my work and in my life do all they can for the young people they love and are invested in. Too many times, those relationships deteriorate, because young people—especially as they become adolescents and young adults—gain control of their physical movements without being able to direct their thoughts and their choices productively. Of course, this is why children need to be taught how to live life from as early an age as possible.

But equal in importance is for young people—especially those who have made mistakes, who find themselves caught in self-destructive patterns, who have not paid enough attention to their instincts or their parents—to realize that the past is no prison. The grace of life begins anew every day. Every sunrise is an opportunity to make new decisions, to walk a new path.

Moving away from a problematic past is not easy. It is not easy to stop smoking, it is not easy to stop procrastinating, it is not easy to learn to be supportive of others if you have not been charitable in the past, it is not easy to live a life of calm if you have spent all your life in chaos. Life is not easy.

We all benefit from learning to recognize who we are, and where our behavior is disconnected from what we know about ourselves. When we hide—behind drink, or drugs, or rudeness, or any other way of disappearing—we make our return to a healthy and productive way of life more difficult.

Human beings are social beings, and are not meant to hide.

The women who loved Carrie were assisted in their search for her by coming to *Judge Hatchett* on television and getting support and guidance with an intervention. Carrie was so far gone, and had hidden from her family and herself for so long, that by the time they found her, she was curled in the most infantile of positions. She had returned herself to a state of total incapacity and dependence. Just like she took herself there—to that most self-destructive place—she can walk herself back into the sunshine of life.

What Carrie has been does not determine who Carrie can be. The same is true of all of us, and all our children. Even if we get locked in a bad pattern for a time, the future will still come to greet us with the dawn of each new day. Dare to stand up and try again when each new day comes to meet you.

Staying locked in a destructive past is a choice and a problem. Life is available to be lived productively, until you are dead. As long as any one of us is breathing, we have the opportunity to live productively and to honor ourselves by making positive choices. Our spirit expects no less from us.

When we do not honor our humanity and make positive choices, our spirit goes silent and we feel abandoned. Feeling abandoned by your own soul cannot help but make you feel dispirited, off balance, and like nothing matters. When we live productively and work toward our goals, when we attend to our talents and our instincts, then our spirit sings. We feel harmony, balance, and possibility. This is the feeling God offers, and the potential for these feelings—harmony, balance, potential, productivity—come packaged as the soul of life.

All of us need to learn from the past, then leave the past where it lives—in the past. Without the constant crippling burden of the past, we can all reach for possibility, we can all stretch for our potential. As Werner Erhard, the American educator, has written, the task before each of us is to "Create your future from your future, not your past."

Consider whether you have self-destructive or self-denying behaviors going on in your life now. Are you depressed? If you are, why? Is it because you would rather be doing a different job than the job you have? Is it because you really wish you'd lose some weight? Are you depressed because you are secretly overspending? Are you depressed because you are hiding something else?

Are you getting high to avoid facing some serious issues in your life? Are you abusive because you have a poor self-image? Are you keeping silent because your secrets are too disturbing to admit?

Are there realities in your life that you feel are "sadly inevitable"? Are there changes you want to make that you are too worried, too low-energy, or too resigned to try? Do you dislike your job and feel like you are unable to change? If you can't change your job, have you considered changing your work? If you can't change your work, have you tried changing your approach to your work? Do you feel reduced about any areas that are ongoing in your life? Were you an active athlete, and now you feel sluggish, like more of a couch potato? Did you take time away from your career, or reduce your responsibilities, and now you want to reenter to be more engaged? To work, to be well paid again?

I challenge you to learn to interpret this resignation, this feeling of inevitability as a cue that it's time to turn worry into positive action. Consider this feeling a blessing, a sign that is guiding you directly to the place you most urgently need to make change.

Today:

Identify one positive choice that you know you need to make in your life right now. Write your choice down. Define one step, however small, that you can take, *today*, to help bring this positive choice into reality in your life. Take this small step, today. Plan another small step for tomorrow, before you close your eyes tonight.

Dare To...

Make new choices.

- Every time you make a choice you don't like, no matter how small, be sure you notice that you're making a choice you don't like.
- Make sure the next choice you make is a positive choice for what you want to achieve.

Move beyond your mistakes.

- Remember that mistakes—and recovery—are part of the human condition. Don't beat yourself up.
- Learn from your errors, so that you can take an active course away from the mistakes you've made in the past.

Live your life in the light of day.

- Realize that hiding suggests shame.
- Understand that shame can be an important signal, and allow yourself to *use* any shame you feel—to provoke you to change the choices you make. Remember: Your past does not have to define your future.

Twelve

Opportunity Knocks.
Will You Answer?

After huge life challenges, traumas, or big dramas, people find the truth harder to hide. An interrupted or troubled life is far more visible than a life that goes on without crisis or strain. My work as a judge often gives me a revealing picture of people, the lives they live, and the troubles they encounter. I have seen thousands of people—young, old, parents, grandparents, aunts, uncles, neighbors, friends—whose lives have been affected and whose hearts have been scarred by trauma or by drama. Sometimes only one or two people are involved; sometimes there are whole families affected, sometimes children, or children and their parents. Sometimes whole communities are torn apart.

Rarely, if ever, is a crisis suffered by one person alone.

In any situation where chaos takes over, days are not predictable, people cannot be depended on, and order does not prevail. Households and families can and do fall apart. People come nearer to court when the strain on family units and social networks increases. Either you find a way to fix the problem, or you may be forced to deal with the court's solution.

People arrive in courtrooms like mine during or in the aftermath of crises. In other words, when people and families and communities can depend on each other to do what they say they will, to do what is expected, to help when the need arises, then calls for intervention are few and the reasons to go to court are minimized. But imagine if you could not depend on your children to go to school, or to stay there once you dropped them off. Perhaps you know this experience. Or imagine a parent who cannot be depended upon to work, or to look for work, to earn money, or to manage the money they are able to get so that their children are fed and have a place to sleep and a place to be nurtured and loved. Perhaps you or someone you know has faced this sad reality.

When we stop investing in our own success, we let our communities and our families down. And most important, we let ourselves down. When we cannot depend on each other, our social and family units falter. No matter what we think or try to convince ourselves to think, "dropping the ball" will have consequences—for us, for our families, for our support networks.

Drama and catastrophe—especially when these crises result from our behavior or poor choices—make us feel bad. We feel bad overall. We feel bad every day. We feel lost, because many times we are losing our bearings, and we are not following our moral compass. Maybe we have lost our sense of direction in life. Maybe we have lost the anchoring support of our family or our friends.

Under these circumstances, too often we do something that is very human (and therefore understandable, even if it's not the right strategy)—we start to make choices that allow us, even temporarily, to forget our longer-term intentions. We focus on feeling "better" in the present. We basically look to do what we can that will seem like a quick fix.

Even though most adults understand that long-term goals require short-term sacrifices, too often we feel so frustrated about what we haven't done, and we focus instead on shorter-term relief. Excessive television. Parties. Drugs. Junk food. Actions of power over others— including physical abuse of spouses, children, even parents. Actions of self-neglect. Anything to distract us, to ease the very real pain we have caused ourselves by not doing what we planned, or by not doing what we know was best for us to do.

The issues that bring people to my courtroom are primarily crippling and destructive life patterns. I see my job as helping them begin to identify new ways to behave, and helping them to state how they'd like for their lives to proceed, according to some new options. I try to help those whom I face in court to learn to live according to their expectations of themselves, so that their life options can improve.

If ever I saw a destructive kid whose future seemed destined by his past, it was Nigel. By age sixteen, when he first appeared in my court, this jaded teen was nearing manhood. He had spent his precious time—his short life—dealing drugs, pimping, and robbing. He was as hard-core as they come. When he came before me, Nigel had already spent two years in various nonconsecutive terms—an eighth of his life—behind bars. He was brought before me by his mom and stepfather. Sadly, he had no relationship with his biological father.

Bright and manipulative, Nigel was a player. He had organized a sophisticated business for himself. In straightforward language, and without a hint of remorse, he explained that when he needed money, he'd simply snatch an old woman's pocketbook. He had no concern for the fact that a grandmother on a fixed income would be severely traumatized and set back by his actions. According to his mother, this teenager was also operating a full-fledged prostitution operation out of a motel and a drug-selling ring. He was methodical and, by street standards, highly successful. He was able to articulate what he was doing and why.

Nigel was all about Nigel, all the time. When I asked where he thought he'd be by age twenty-five, Nigel nonchalantly answered, "Probably dead." So his sense of a limited life expectancy contributed to his willingness to perform reckless, callous actions.

After about five minutes of listening to Nigel talk about Nigel, my blood began to boil. Uncharacteristically, I let it show. I was disgusted and furious.

"What the hell is wrong with you, Nigel?" I asked, in a tone closer to a shout than befits a judge.

"Well, you tell me how a young black man is supposed to survive in this country, Judge?" he retorted, smirking. "I got nobody to support me." This was an outrageous claim, especially since the child's caring but frustrated mother was standing just a few feet away.

"Don't you dare give me that 'my mama don't care' stuff, young man. And how dare you continue to poison our community with drugs and prostitutes! Bailiff—get him out of here!"

Even while I was seething, I had my first idea for an intervention with Nigel. His communication skills and his "success" showed that he had brains; he had potential. This kid was so far gone, I didn't know if it would work. But I knew I had to try.

My plan was to engage the youngest daughter of Dr. Martin Luther King Jr., Elder Bernice A. King, an ordained minister. Bernice was my first law clerk at Fulton County Juvenile Court. A law clerk primarily does legal research for judges. But during and after her time as a court clerk with me, Bernice King did a lot of work helping me to develop creative, effective programs to get and keep kids on the right path. Bernice had worked with Dr. Johnnetta Cole, who was president of Spelman College at the time, to develop a network called S.I.S.—Sisters Inspire Success. This was a fabulous program that partnered young girls who were in foster care and who had the potential to aim for high goals with young women students at Spelman. Bernice already understood the nature of intervention that had become my trademark.

Opportunity Only Knocks

When I called to tell Bernice what I had in mind, she agreed to get involved with this teenager, who desperately needed to see another side of life, the real face of success, and the truth of sacrifice. I sent Nigel to Atlanta, where Bernice met him at the King Center, the final resting place of Dr. King and a national hub for education about nonviolent social change. The videotape shows Bernice escorting this recalcitrant teenager through the King Center, talking about the civil rights movement and her father's Nobel Prize. She remains gracious, as if she's welcoming an honored guest. Nigel goes along, but his attitude is nonchalant, and his swagger speaks volumes.

The goal was to show Nigel the incredible sacrifices made by those who have gone before him. Some of the great work others have done has been to fight against the very suffering and devastation he was bringing into his community. If this kid really grasped his history, could he dare continue on this path of terror and destruction? If he truly understood his history, would he throw away his future? Nigel's clear intelligence and his ability to make intellectual connections was key to the response I hoped he'd have to this intervention.

What I didn't know was that at that time, the center was hosting an exhibit on lynching—there were photographs and summaries that gave a raw and powerful portrayal of Jim Crow at its very worst. Bernice led him through that exhibit as well. All of their exchanges were captured on videotape. As they passed through image after image of African Americans hanged bleeding and dying, Nigel got sad and serious.

He walked increasingly slowly, and suddenly, hand clasped to his mouth, Nigel—the pimp, the drug dealer, the thief, the I-don't-give-a-damn hard-core teen—ran for the center's main door. He was visibly ill, made nauseous by the recorded truth.

That was how he spent his morning in Atlanta. So far so good.

For Nigel's afternoon on that same day, I had called on an old and trusted friend, Reverend C. T. Vivian. Reverend Vivian was also one of Dr. Martin Luther King's lieutenants, and was himself a towering figure in the struggle for civil rights. Incredibly, Reverend Vivian left his wife's hospital bed to meet Bernice and Nigel at the King Center—that's how determined he was to support me and to make a difference for a boy reaching the end of his childhood.

Reverend Vivian and Nigel talked a little, and then they went into the center's offices, where he showed a video of himself being beaten on the courthouse steps in Selma, Alabama, as he tried to register to vote in 1965. Nigel was too young to know firsthand the historic story the footage was telling, but he watched and listened, and seemed to perceive that he was in the presence of a hero and a righteous man. This graphic imagery showed Reverend Vivian and other voter-rights activists confronted by a racist sheriff and his entourage, not because they had stolen a grandmother's purse or trafficked in drugs, but beaten only for the color of their skin and for their fundamental desire to exercise their legal right to vote.

When the video ended, Reverend Vivian returned to the image of the sheriff raising his hand to strike him. This peaceful pastor then turned and said to Nigel, "Son, I took that beating so you wouldn't have to." Speaking barely above a whisper, tears in his eyes, Reverend C. T. Vivian added, "Nigel, what Judge Hatchett tells me you've been doing to our community—prostituting women, pouring drugs into our citizens, and stealing from old people—makes me wonder if all the beatings and the jail time and the heartache we endured were worth the struggle."

With these words, I'm told a visible change came over Nigel. It's hard to detect where it came from—his posture, his facial expression, maybe from somewhere within. But Reverend Vivian and Bernice King believed that their time with Nigel had an impact. I appreciated their efforts, and I hoped that the exposure to righteous struggle and being in the presence of true heroes would implant new, different, and useful ideas in Nigel's mind.

I planned to move forward with Nigel from there.

Nigel returned to New York, where he appeared before me again for the closing segment of the intervention. Together, we watched the video of his visit to the King Center. It was difficult to watch—from his sickened reaction to the lynching photos to the senseless beatings of a nonviolent activist.

"Nigel," I reminded him, "when you were in my courtroom a few days ago, you told me you pictured yourself dead by age twenty-five."

"Judge, I don't know what you're talking about," he responded. At first I thought this was a typical smartass remark, and I mentally prepared my retort. But he continued. "Judge, that person no longer exists." This time, I remained silent as Nigel went on with his clear speech, describing how what he had seen had changed him and how he planned to reinvent himself. As I listened to him, I remained convinced that he needed to prove himself, but I also was reaffirmed in my assessment of his intelligence. He got the point and made the leap: reinvention is the name of the life improvement game.

Nigel's story does not end there. He did make progress, but in fits and starts. We went to some pretty incredible lengths for this young man, initially arranging for him to be mentored by Dean Alvin Darden of Morehouse College, even helping him get into a private high school out of state, which he promptly dropped out of. His adjustment did not happen in a straight line, in spite of his good mind.

Nigel returned to the court a few years later and we addressed his progress. I told him I still believed in him, that I still believed in hope. But I made sure he understood that only Nigel could control the direction of his life. I required that he accept another mentorship period, and as he stood in the courtroom I introduced by satellite the right men for the job. At a conference table sat several members of 100 Black Men of Atlanta, the local chapter of an elite national organization with chapters across the country and abroad. Several of these men are friends of mine, and every one is incredibly accomplished and well-respected.

I wanted Nigel to see what strong black men look like. I wanted him to see men being able to legitimately form businesses and thrive, and being able to give back to their communities. Among them was Tommy Dortch, who has been a close friend and confidant to me for decades; he is a prominent businessman and Chair Emeritus of 100 Black Men of America. There was also John Grant, Bernard Porché, Darrell Fitzgerald, John Hammond, and William Stanley. William was my play "big brother" in high school, and he and his wife are the godparents of my two sons, so you know how deeply I value Billy and his wife, Ivenue. I have long-term and wonderful relationships with all of these men, and I've called on them more times than I can count.

These men are at the top of their game, and they did not get there by lying, cheating, drugging, or pimping. They are playing a game that you cannot play if you commit street crimes, if you don't value your mind enough to use it productively. Since my goal is to redirect lives that might otherwise be wasted, and since this is the community of my support team in Atlanta, these are the heavy hitters I called in. I wanted Nigel to see and feel real power and success.

Of course, these men became involved because I called, but their commitment to nurturing the young people in our community has been consistent. The 100 has sponsored and sent hundreds of kids to college. We are all operating under the direction of the United Negro College Fund's striking and memorable affirmation: "A mind is a terrible thing to waste."

This amazing group of righteous individuals, who have built global businesses and global reputations, agreed to gather together and speak to Nigel to see if there was some way they could help. During their talk, Tommy Dortch invited Nigel to come visit at his office. At Tommy's office in Peachtree Center, Nigel would see an important success story. He would see what Tommy Dortch had built—without selling drugs, without prostituting women, without destroying our communities.

All of us could see that Nigel had a very good mind. We were trying, at really the last moments of his childhood, to see if we could expose him to realities and behaviors that would be legitimate, constructive, and productive.

Ultimately, Nigel apprenticed with Tommy Dortch, who was able to expose him to building a successful business without threat or worry from the law.

Nigel's road to redemption continued to be marked by setbacks and stumbles. At first he was not able to keep the faith, and he did not report to work every day, as he had promised. This failure to report to his job violated his probation, and so I required him to turn himself in to the authorities. He did, and served a few months in jail. Although he was not able to walk the line the first time, Tommy Dortch allowed him to return to his "internship," in the hopes that the time he served would make him hungrier for a clean break.

A period followed where I could faithfully (and happily) report that Nigel was creating a future incredibly different from his past. I'm also, however, enough of a realist to know that his recalibration of his life was a fragile process. I hoped and prayed that the experience I had worked so diligently to arrange for him would keep him focused and purposeful about the choices he made and his potential to have a productive life.

The current report I have on Nigel is not good. Three or four times, after he failed to live up to his agreements, he was given second chances. But Tommy Dortch's staff reported that Nigel could not maintain any responsible posture toward working, and repeatedly demonstrated that he would not follow through on his stated commitment to his job and his goals. Nigel was given opportunities that other, much more dedicated young people would have run with, and potentially leveraged themselves to the highest heights. But Nigel proved himself unable to even understand his enormous good fortune. Many young men never even get close to the caliber of professional of a Tommy Dortch or a William Stanley. Many young men and women never get a second chance. None of us wanted to see Nigel fail, and looking back, I can see that my associates and I were working extra hard to keep him from failing, since we had given him access enough to support success. We all wanted him to be successful!

Nigel did not come to my attention until he was almost grown; he was in his teenage years when he arrived in my courtroom. Apparently, for Nigel, seventeen or eighteen was too late to instill a sense of working toward a larger goal. He was accustomed to working toward an immediate end; he could not see the fruit that would come in the next season. He could not dare bring himself to want legitimacy enough to devote himself to his opportunities. And so he was unable to benefit from the opportunities the intervention arranged for him.

At this point, Nigel's intervention is done. There will be no more second chances, no more new arrangements. From my perspective, we lost Nigel. Or, more accurately, Nigel lost himself.

Honestly, Nigel's inability to respond to an important opportunity is not that unusual a story. Just because opportunity knocks doesn't mean that the door gets flung open. Not everyone is ready when opportunity arrives. Not everyone can hear the rap at the door. Anything from distraction to depression can keep you from hearing it. So, the question—*will you answer?*—is very real. Most young men in Nigel's circumstances are not afforded such special chances to try again.

Think through the opportunities you'd like to have arrive at your doorstep. And prepare yourself, now, to respond to the opportunity you dream of. We have got to be prepared to take advantage of opportunity. Like Nigel, we can still lose out if we don't make ourselves ready and if we don't respond eagerly and with determination.

Opportunity only knocks; it does nothing further for you. Making the most of opportunity is our responsibility.

Children have to be taught how to live from the beginning of their lives. They need to learn what's appropriate from their youngest years. They need to also learn that life and learning is not always comfortable. Not only did Nigel not see himself as bigger than his failures, but it seems that he could not really acknowledge the failure in his actions at all. I suspect he felt safer and more powerful where he was a "player," and that outside his comfort zone he felt too unsure. But if you operate solely from your comfort zone, you are probably not doing enough to make progress.

Nigel was so accustomed to trouble that trouble became what he sought in life. All he could think about was the moment in front of him. He was not able to think about his future, and to take steps now that would make his future better, even when he was presented with a near-miraculous series of opportunities. He returned himself to a life expectancy of twenty-five, by returning to the drama and violence of the streets. He accepted the invitation, but by his own choice refused to do what was required to stay.

Each one of us is in charge of how we are defined. Nobody can tell us who we are. Even if we have stumbled, failed, created catastrophe— every new day provides a new chance for good. If you go to bed tonight deciding that you will stop being self-destructive, that does not mean that when you wake tomorrow, your task will be easy. But when you wake tomorrow, your task will be defined. You can define you.

The good news is if we train ourselves to expect accomplishment, to expect success, to expect progress, we can discipline ourselves in our lives, and devote our time and energies to achieving our expectations.

The Solution

The business of life, and the business of righting your life, requires deciding on your vision, making a plan to support that vision, and keeping pace with your plan. Taking these steps is the way to recover from the mistakes and mishaps of the past.

Making a new plan sometimes requires that you develop a new vision. Other times no new vision is required: developing a new plan really means outlining, step by step, a vision you already have but have not yet been able to achieve.

When I was sworn in as a judge, I promised myself to keep cultivating "vision" every day I sat on the bench. I promised myself I would look for potential in everyone no matter what in their past had brought them to the courtroom. I not only was sworn in as an official of the court, but I swore to myself that I would envision a new start for every person who came before me.

This is the spirit that permitted me to develop an intervention and opportunities for Nigel, and so many persons I've encountered in my court. Young people tug at my heart especially. I am always willing to try as many ideas as I can to see if something can put a young person on the path to self-definition and self-respect.

The effort to try to see a new start for every person I serve helps keep me fresh and inventive on the bench. The day I can no longer operate from a place of envisioning hope and defining new chances is the day I will step down. The most I have to offer is to help others determine how to begin again. *My job is not to fix people. My job is to empower them to fix themselves.*

Think what you or your child would have done with Nigel's intervention, with those stunning opportunities. Consider every day that you wake up to a stunning opportunity. Life is not promised; the future is not promised. When you receive the grace of a new day, you are given a gift that not everyone gets. Each one of us gains new opportunities every time we witness daylight. Think about how you can make the opportunity of every day turn into the opportunity of a lifetime. When opportunity knocks, do you answer?

Today:

Consider your situation—is there something that you dare to do or change in your life? An action that moves you out of your comfort zone into a fulfilling new direction? Write it down. Then make a note of three things you need to do to make the most of this opportunity, and do one of them today.

Dare To...

Expect that options for positive change will arrive in your life.

- Be vigilant about recognizing when possibilities present themselves.
- Be relentless about moving in a more positive direction.

Do the most you can with the one life you have.

- Seize your future potential by not letting your past hold tomorrow hostage.
- See new opportunities for what they are: a chance for you to move beyond old mishaps into new possibilities.

Crack the code of life: learn what success requires.

- Make sure you are pursuing goals that matter to you.
- Want enough from life that you will work tirelessly toward righteous and rewarding goals.

Thirteen

New Hope Road

My fabulous Aunt Ruth was an amazing spirit. She was in love with life. Aunt Ruth was seven years older than my mother, and they were two of six girls in a family of nine children, Aunt Ruth the third sister and my mother the sixth. The last time I went to see Aunt Ruth before she died, she was still giving me important advice. She told me I needed to live my life so that, looking back, I would not have any regrets. She cautioned me that I worked too hard; she wanted me to be sure that I had enough fun before I got too old to have fun. When I tried to leave her eightieth birthday party at 2:30 a.m. to go to bed, she admonished me: "Glenda, you can sleep when you're dead."

Her daughter, my older cousin Lenolia Keith Bryant, is very much like her mother was—glamorous and flamboyant. No doubt, my appreciation for Aunt Ruth made me love Lenolia all the more. Her South Carolina accent sounds melodic and emphatic. Her favorite saying is, "Don't give up. Don't give in. And whatever you do, don't give out." Lenolia has a way of singing the words as she speaks them. As I grew older, I came to appreciate the meaning of the words as well as their sound, especially the way they challenged me to never even *consider* giving up.

I have thought of my cousin's advice countless times over the years. It is assertive, urging us to persist, to insist, to *keep going*—as we work toward what we know is important to us.

I have been blessed to be able to see the other side of a decision or an opportunity. It's my job to symbolically stand in the gap between the reality of the present and the potential future, to help those who cannot see beyond immediate circumstances. I can see across the divide to the other side, a place I like to call "New Hope Road," a place with new possibilities. A higher ground where you can claim your vision. This is the gift I share in my courtroom and in my life. One experience in my courtroom vividly brought Lenolia's directive, once again, to life.

Courage

Pamela, a warm-eyed young teenager, bravely made her way to my TV courtroom to get what she believed was rightly hers. At just eighteen years old, and virtually alone in the world, Pamela came seeking justice, and she left with a whole lot more.

Pamela never knew her biological mother, who lost custody when Pamela was still an infant. She was soon adopted by Martine, a single woman with no other children.

Sadly, when Pamela was seventeen, Martine died, leaving the teenager without family. Martine's relatives, the only family Pamela had known, had never really accepted her. These were people who apparently believed that if you weren't "blood," you weren't really family.

Once Martine died, Pamela became an orphan again. This time, however, she was entitled to Social Security benefits. When Pamela learned that the money due her was going into the hands of her late mother's family, she had to take action. She contacted the *Judge Hatchett* show about suing this very unfamily-like family for the benefits due to her after her adoptive mother's death.

I remember asking Pamela months later where she had found the courage to take this big, potentially risky step all by herself. She said she had watched the show for a long time and felt as if she knew me. "You gave me strength because I believed in you. I saw you help others, and always believed you could help me."

Strong, determined, and alone, Pamela just said no to those who tried to divert her from seeking justice by warning her against airing "dirty family laundry" on TV. The legality of the case was straightforward—the Social Security benefits were legally hers. But the emotions and tensions swirling around this situation were more complicated than the law.

I entered judgment in Pamela's favor, and ordered the family members to return the Social Security benefits to her. The decision coincided with a break in the taping. I got up to return to chambers, and as I did, I saw that Pamela remained in her seat, looking frightened, like a deer in headlights.

Despite the verdict in her favor, Pamela seemed to feel no joy. The relief of resolution did not even show on her face. Instead, the girl sat motionless, as if she was waiting for someone to tell her what to do next.

My intuition urged me not to walk by that scared and lonely girl, and that quiet inner voice should not be ignored. So often we hear people say they did something because they had a "hunch." Well, that's intuition talking. Our intuition knows us, and participates in our lives with us. *Our intuition will guide us, if we are open, if we get quiet enough to hear.*

I stopped, extended my hand, and asked Pamela if she'd like to follow me. She seemed glad to have someplace to go. I wasn't sure what would happen next, but I knew I was doing what I should.

I closed the door behind us and we sat quietly for a long minute. I looked into her eyes and, for a brief second, into her young and troubled soul.

"Pamela, what's going on in your life? Where are you headed after you leave here today?" Pamela did not have an answer, so I continued talking quietly, asking a few other questions, trying to determine which answers, which plans the child had. Before me in my chambers was the classic motherless child. A child without a parent *and* without a plan. My intuition was proving that I was right to spend more time with Pamela.

"Pamela," I asked, "can you tell me what your dream is for your life? If you could do anything at all in the world, what would that be?" She answered honestly that she just was not sure. I reassured her that there was nothing wrong with not knowing exactly where she was headed. I suggested that I might be able to help her get the tools that would help her figure it out.

I had some ideas, but I was most concerned about her immediate well-being. Certainly I could not "fix" Pamela's family. There was no question that the verdict in the courtroom meant the end of any relationship with Martine's relatives. And even though I longed to repair these frayed ties, it was not possible. Their theft of Pamela's resources, and their unwillingness to enfold her—that was enough to require that I think about other possibilities. If I was going to help Pamela, something would have to happen that didn't involve this "adoptive family." Pamela seemed to have had enough of them as well. No one expects to have to sue their own family.

Pamela had graduated from high school the previous month and was working part-time. But she had absolutely no plan for her future.

She was traumatized, and in mourning for the only mother she'd ever known.

Pamela's life was characterized by loss and chaos. How in the world was this girl going to get by alone? What street corner might she land on? What roof would cover her head? What could I do to help her find the emotional space to begin to dream? What could I arrange to help a parentless child sent too early in the world alone?

Pamela was like too many young people I'd seen, hovering between wise and unwise decisions. One step in the wrong direction could mean the difference between a productive future and subsequent visits to court, or worse. Pamela's circumstances could easily and drastically decline. She seemed to sense this as she told me about some of the "friends" she'd been hanging out with. They didn't seem like friends at all, but other lost young people offering her some marginal connection and a sense of belonging. The likelihood that they would lead her to bad choices seemed high.

It became apparent as we talked that my chambers represented a safe haven for Pamela—maybe the only safe place she had at the time. Sitting at my desk, my robe flung over the chair, the formal "judge/plaintiff" relationship was finished for the two of us. There we were together, facing a whole lot of unanswered questions. Had she walked out of the courtroom instead of visiting my chambers that day, I can only imagine the path she might have pursued. I simply could not let this girl return home alone. I could not leave her to the incredibly uncertain future.

"Pamela," I asked, "what if there was a way for you to attend college starting in September? Would you be able to buckle down and make it work? I think I could help you get in, but you'd have to focus and work really hard to get yourself out."

She stared at me, shocked and silent, bending forward to better understand exactly what I was saying. She nodded, slowly at first, then more emphatically as her eyes filled with water. "Are you kidding? I really want to go to college. But Judge, can you really do this for me? I don't have the money. Would you help me?"

"Yes, I will," I told her. Pamela sat wordless as I picked up the phone and called an old friend.

College

Bob Whitehead answered his phone on the first ring. I had met Bob years ago when I served as judge of Fulton County Juvenile Court in Atlanta. After reading about one of my really tough cases in the newspaper, Bob, then a complete stranger, called my office. He left a message with my secretary, something about knowing my family and wanting to send the troubled child he had read about to college!

At first I dismissed it, thinking it might have been another crank call, but then he called back, and I decided to check him out. My mother confirmed that she and my daddy had in fact known Bob Whitehead for years through his local floral business. "You make that call, honey," my mother advised. Of course I did.

I learned that Bob, a retired Atlanta flower-shop owner, was an alumnus of Livingstone College in Salisbury, North Carolina, one of the country's Historically Black Colleges and Universities. Bob is certainly no millionaire, but he has an enormous heart and has sent many deserving kids to college, paying their way out of his own pocket. After Bob sent the boy from my courtroom to college we stayed in close contact.

There are people who talk a great deal about what should be done to protect children at risk. Then there are the Bob Whiteheads of the world, who do something about the problems they see.

He does not seek money from foundations or grants; rather, he writes the checks from his own bank account. Bob lives the adage that if you give a person a fish, you feed him or her for a day. But if you *teach* that person to fish, you provide food for a lifetime. I thank God for Bob Whitehead, a modest and yet phenomenal unsung hero.

With Pamela watching in silence as I spoke on the phone, I told Bob her story. He immediately agreed that Pamela sounded like the kind of student he'd like to sponsor. And he believed she could get into Livingstone despite the late date.

When I hung up and told Pamela what Bob had proposed, she got that shell-shocked look again. "Judge, are you serious? You mean this man wants to send me to college even though he's never met me?"

"That's right," I answered, never ceasing to be amazed by Bob's grace and generosity as I watched the miracle unfolding in front of my eyes. We hugged, and in that embrace I tried to convey all my hopes and dreams for this deserving girl.

Picture the scene. A teenager whose adoptive family had taken her only source of funds is suddenly facing the possibility that a generous stranger wants to pay to send her to college. As I watched, Pamela seemed to become infused with hope. I could already see a change in her and it was wonderful. But there was little time to linger feeling warm and charmed; we had work to do.

Bob worked his magic with the admissions office at Livingstone. I did what I could from my end, helping Pamela wrap up her legal affairs and offering guidance about the road ahead.

It wasn't lost on me that I was asking a great deal of this girl. Going to college would be potentially life-changing for Pamela. But it would require that she make some serious sacrifices. It would mean uprooting herself from a big, familiar city and planting herself in a small, unknown southern town where she didn't know a soul.

I warned Pamela that she might be tempted to give up, especially when things got tough. I told her emphatically that her job was to fight against that temptation. I told her what I have told thousands of young people: "I am pulling for you. And I expect greatness."

And then I repeated what my cousin Lenolia had said so many times: "Pamela," I said. "Don't give up. Don't give in. And whatever you do, don't give out."

There's another incredible part to this story. Across the country from Pamela, at home in Seattle, a woman named Wanda watched Pamela's appearance on my show. She rarely saw the show, but was home sick that day with a bad cold.

When Pamela and her estranged "family members" appeared, Wanda saw someone she thought she knew. Alone in the house, she suddenly began to scream, "That's my child. That's my baby girl. That's her. I know it is!"

Immediately, she called to tell a couple of friends. They were doubtful, and wondered whether she had lost it. Of course, Wanda's friends thought the girl on the show wasn't her child, or if it was, how could Wanda possibly know? Wanda did not recognize the girl's first or last name. Both had changed when she was adopted. And she had last seen the child at about three months of age. How could she possibly know this was her daughter? On television? On any old weekday? What were the chances?

Wanda hung up from the chorus of doubters and called two other people, her two daughters who live together in the Midwest, to tell them who she believed she had seen. They reminded her that *Judge Hatchett* aired earlier, and they had missed it. As the girls listened to their mother, they too became concerned about her, and worried about the possibility that she had relapsed after years of sobriety.

But Wanda insisted in that protective, maternal way women have when it's about their children: "I'm not crazy. I'm telling you the girl on that show is my daughter. I know it as sure as I know anything, and I'm going to find her!" Wanda was alone in feeling certain. Everyone doubted her, but her intuition spurred her on.

With nowhere else to turn she decided to write me to learn how she could find out if this could be her daughter. But sadly, so sadly, I never received Wanda's letters. I don't know if they ever arrived, or were possibly misplaced. That I never knew she was reaching out troubled me in retrospect, because I would have been so eager to help. As it was, I had no idea about Wanda's attempt to locate Pamela.

Without hearing from me, Wanda continued to desperately try to find a way to reach the girl she saw on *Judge Hatchett*.

Pamela had marched forward from my courtroom with remarkable inventiveness and determination. While we were working to change her circumstances, to set her life on a new course, she took another huge leap. She set out to see if she could find her biological family, contacting the authorities about opening her adoption record.

As you're beginning to see, Pamela is someone who has the "don't give up" thing deep inside. Through her research, she learned the address of the apartment where her biological mother lived at the time of her birth.

Once the record was opened, Pamela went to the last known address listed for her mother, the place she had been living at the time she lost custody of baby Pamela.

Pamela knocked on the door of the apartment, hopeful but unsure of what she would find there. She introduced herself to the two young women who answered, explaining that she was searching for her birth mother who once lived at that address. Within seconds it was clear that prayers had been answered.

The women at the door were Pamela's older sisters. They started to scream and cry, hugging Pamela and dragging her inside the apartment while curious onlookers gathered in the hallway.

"Mama was right! Nobody believed her when she kept saying it. You *do* exist. My God, Mama was right!" The sisters immediately got their mother on the phone from Seattle and the screaming and tears began all over again.

When everyone settled down, Pamela asked Wanda a very simple question: "How did you know it was me?"

"Honey, I just knew—you look just like me!" Wanda answered. By this time, Pamela was holding a photo of their mother and she could see the resemblance herself.

Pamela simply would not give up. She would not give in. And she would not give out. Just like Cousin Lenolia said. Young, knocked around in life, but soaring with spirit, Pamela persisted. And just as I couldn't picture giving up on Pamela, neither could she imagine giving up on herself.

Twice I had seen this tough young woman stand up for herself—demanding justice from her adopted mother's family and pursuing the search for her birth family in the face of unbelievable obstacles.

Reunion

Today, the women are a family of four. Pamela was so grateful for the efforts Bob Whitehead and I had made on her behalf. More than once she told me, "Judge, you saved my life."

So when she wrote to tell me that she was completing her work at Livingstone that spring, I simply couldn't stay away.

I decided to surprise her on graduation day, but I talked with Bob, the real guardian angel in this story, to let him know I planned to come. Graciously, the president of the university invited me to walk with the graduates and even briefly address them.

I arrived in a big, hard-to-miss black SUV and scooted out of the car and away from my security detail as the student processional made its way through campus. I was so proud as I scanned the students in their caps and gowns.

Pamela spied me first and broke out of the line to wrap me in a huge hug. As she pulled back and looked at me I saw it again—the astonished look I'd first seen in my chambers the day I heard her case. But this time it was followed by a big, beautiful, confident smile.

The Pamela I saw on graduation day was an accomplished young adult, heading for a career in social work. The girl who'd taken slow, halting steps in my chamber four years before now walked with confidence to claim the diploma she had rightfully earned. This was the first time I'd seen her in four years and the change was remarkable.

Pamela's journey through college was difficult for her. But she dedicated herself to her studies, learned a great deal about herself, and was by any definition a huge success in spite of huge obstacles.

I briefly addressed the graduating class before the commencement speaker; emotions took hold of me as I shared with the audience the remarkable story of this phenomenal young woman's journey. It started in my courtroom, and how poetic that this chapter of her story would end at her commencement.

While I was speaking, Pamela stood up from her seat, made her way through her fellow classmates, and rushed to embrace me on the stage. At that point I gestured for Bob Whitehead to join us because it was his generosity that made this moment possible. While we embraced, the audience jumped to their feet with thunderous applause as they joined in this sacred moment of celebration. Perhaps on some level they could really appreciate the miraculous journey and the fact that she never gave in, she never gave up, and she never gave out. As Bob, Pamela, and I stood in this circle, this emotional embrace, I thought back to my courtroom, to my intuition speaking. What would have happened if I hadn't listened, if I had not reached out to touch her, to try and help her?

Doing just enough was not enough for me. I couldn't give up on this shell-shocked and orphaned teenager. And I couldn't give in to the minimal requirements once a verdict was reached, leaving her with no guidance and no help. In that split second when I started to leave the courtroom, I was compelled to act. The opportunity presented itself and had I not stood up to the challenge, who knows what might have happened? *Intuition speaks to all of us, and we must dare to listen.*

The same is true of Pamela. Opportunity presented itself. And what about Pamela's great leap of faith? She stepped out on belief by saying yes to an unfamiliar, intimidating world. In that moment she changed the course of her life. Unwilling to give up on justice, unwilling to give up on her birth family, and unwilling to give up on herself, Pamela manifested huge blessings, one after the other.

"If it hadn't been for you and Mr. Whitehead," Pamela later told me, "I really might have been in serious trouble. I was running with the wrong crowd and God knows I could have become a drug addict, gang member, or worse." She said I had saved her life. But in fact I had simply given her a way out; it was her choice to grab hold of the lifeline and tug on it.

Pamela needed something and someone to hold on to. I couldn't create an instant family for this lonely girl. But I could reach out with a helping hand. Blessed by the incredible generosity of Bob Whitehead and embraced by the nurturing students and faculty at Livingstone, Pamela made it her business to benefit from the opportunity of a lifetime.

Now Pamela plans on a career of service to others. Her dream is to develop a transitional house for young teenage girls who are drifting or are trying to find their way without adequate adult support.

The challenge you face may not be as dramatic as Pamela's. Most of us will never be deliberately harmed by relatives. Most of us never feel the loneliness that comes from being without parents, without families. But all of us will face other difficulties—finding a job that pays the bills, caring for elderly parents, finding fulfilling work to do, forgiving ourselves for poor choices.

What about you? When is the last time you refused to give in to your doubts, fears, or insecurities? What do you remember about a split second when you faced a decision that may have changed your life? Did you dare to make the courageous decision; did you say yes to yourself, or were you too afraid to branch out in a new direction? Is your intuition urging you to take action?

Are you in a personal relationship that has gone to hell—where you are not loved and respected but you are still hanging on? Are you in a job that does not challenge you? Perhaps you have wanted to adopt a baby and you hesitate to submit the application? Perhaps you want to go back to school, or perhaps you want to move and live in a foreign country? Have you always wanted to know your biological father and your fear of further rejection has kept you from finding and communicating with him? What new road awaits you? What does your inner voice have to say?

Today:

Are you at an important crossroad in your life today? Do you have the courage to turn onto New Hope Road? If not, what is stopping you? What is your inner voice telling you to do? Take time today to get quiet and listen very carefully to your inner voice for direction.

Dare To...

Believe in you.

- Trust your instincts to lead you to action.
- Don't let the actions of others keep you from living a fulfilling life.

Listen to your inner voice.

- Be a partner to the voice that speaks within you.
- Cherish good opportunities enough that you don't let them pass you by.

Step up to your future.

- Dare to do what's difficult, and reap those rewards.
- Go down a road you haven't traveled before. Walk down your own "New Hope Road."

Fourteen

Claim Your Healing

Proverbs and old sayings carry centuries of wisdom, distilled into forms we can remember and quote. The sayings that people know and live by reveal much about their experience, character, and beliefs. My mother, Clemmie Barnes Hatchett, is one of the most spirited people on the planet. She is also an optimist of the highest order. The proverbial question, "Is the glass half empty or half full?" is a question my mother will always answer the same way. If a glass contains barely a drop of liquid, my mother will call it a glass half full. I have a friend and colleague, Judge Joyce London Alexander, whose mother's response to the empty glass debate is, "No matter, just fill the glass up!"

Are you a person who sees the glass as half empty, focusing on what is lacking? Are you a person who sees the glass as half full, which is optimistic, but is only an observation? Or are you, like Judge Alexander's mother, *active* and prepared to fill the glass, whatever its condition?

Many of us meet people every day who view their glass as empty and don't think twice about filling it. The empty glass is daunting and can be dangerous, but the empty "spiritual glass" needs filling nonetheless.

Hope Eternal

My mother has always been within reach, although she wanted me to learn to be fully independent. No one has taught me more about the importance of believing in a brighter tomorrow. I want to share with you one inspiring example of my mother's unwavering belief.

About ten months after my father died, our family was still going through a raw and difficult time when I drove to Nashville for a meeting of the National Council of Juvenile and Family Court Judges with my sons and my mother, who I had suggested should join us because I figured she could use a change of scenery. We all looked forward to the time together.

After a couple of days of work for me and fun for the family, the meeting came to a close with a dinner dance on Friday evening. These events are usually very enjoyable, especially since the boys and my mom have met quite a few of my colleagues over the years. In fact, many of my colleagues lovingly call her "Mama Judge."

As we were rushing to shower and dress, Mama announced that she didn't feel well and would prefer to rest in the room. I figured she was just tired from all the running around and encouraged her to come along.

"Mama, you know you always love these things once you get there. They're planning a wonderful dinner and you'll have fun dancing with all my colleagues. Come with us, please?"

She agreed without too much effort on my part. My mother rarely admits to feeling tired and thrives on the high-energy image she projects. She finished dressing, donning a stunning cocktail suit and her best earrings, and off we went.

It really was a lovely evening. Everyone made an appropriate fuss over Mama. As promised, she danced with several of my male colleagues. The food was fabulous, and I enjoyed visiting with fellow judges I see only a couple of times a year. I felt like I had made the right decision encouraging Mama to come along with us.

By around eleven, I was exhausted and couldn't wait to get to my fluffy hotel bed. I found Mama, who had resisted coming, still going strong on the dance floor.

We returned to our table and started gathering our things when, out of the blue, Mama fell onto the table, face first! Luckily, most things had been cleared, so she avoided cutting herself on silverware or a glass. But to see my mother fall forward was an enormously scary sight.

By the time someone called 911, my mom had come to and seemed cogent. Mama is allergic to alcohol and seafood. Although I am super careful to check everything she eats when we are out, I guessed that the salad might have had an anchovy dressing. However, her symptoms were usually not this severe.

Paramedics arrived quickly, checked her vital signs, and carried Mama out of the ballroom on a stretcher. I sent a dear friend and colleague, Judge Veronica Morgan-Price, to tell the boys what had happened and to stay with my sons while we headed for the emergency room. I'd call them as soon as I knew something.

As we were getting loaded into the ambulance, the driver asked where I'd like Mama to be taken. I hadn't a clue. "If this was your mom, where would you take *her*?" I asked. His answer sent us speeding off to Vanderbilt Medical Center. Even though I was sure that this was probably an exaggerated allergic reaction, the idea of the Vanderbilt Medical

Center was comforting. I figured Mama would get some medicine, a thorough checkup, and we'd be back at the hotel within a few hours.

During the ride I shifted into "command and control" mode and started furiously making calls on my cell phone. Glenda the "get-it-done daughter" was in full swing. I reached my two brothers and suggested that they drive up to Nashville in the morning and drive my car back with the boys. I'd fly Mama home so she could avoid the drive, which took several hours.

"Yes," I said with big-sister confidence left over from the days when I really did consider myself older and wiser. "Mama's fine, I'm sure they'll keep her for observation for a few hours, but there's nothing to worry about."

We were seen quickly at the hospital. Between us, Mama and I managed to answer three sets of the same questions about her medical history. Yes, she was basically a very healthy grandmother, who took almost no medication but did have this nasty pair of allergies. Yes, no, about ten months ago, happens occasionally, lives alone, three times a day, alcohol and seafood.

The doctors tested and conferred. We waited and waited. Then the chief resident came in and pulled the privacy curtain behind him. He didn't hold back, looking from Mama to me. "Mrs. Hatchett, Judge, we've got a serious problem here."

I was listening intently as the doctor described my mother's most worrisome symptom, blood in the spinal fluid. He believed it indicated a cerebral aneurysm, and with a degree of nonchalance that made my blood boil, he announced, "I'm not a bit sure she'll make it through the night. We think there's been some hemorrhaging on the brain." He seemed to be speaking as if my mother had already expired. An aneurysm is basically a weakness in the wall of a brain artery or vein, which causes a ballooning of the blood vessel. Without repair, it can be fatal.

Having dropped this bombshell, this young, insensitive, no-bedside-manner doctor turned to us and said, "The chief neurologist will have to see your mother when he makes his rounds tomorrow. I don't want to wake him now." Then he turned and left the tiny room.

Dumbfounded, I ran after him. I stopped him as he prepared to enter another patient's cubicle. "Doctor, what exactly are you talking about here? You've suggested my mother may not live through the night, and you're worried about waking the chief neurologist? You will either call this doctor—*now*—or I will do it for you!"

So picture this, if you will. I'm in my fabulous after-five attire, tugging on the sleeve of this upstart physician who has shown no signs of humanity in the fifteen minutes we've spent with him. I've started to churn inside. Things are sounding dire and, what's more, it's the first time since my dad's death that I've been in a hospital. The memories are not good ones.

In the past, our family dynamic was that Dad would be the one in charge in times of crisis. For many years I had been his backup and was just fine with that role. But suddenly things had changed. Feeling oh so alone, I realized that with Dad no longer with us, it was up to me to do the heavy lifting.

I immediately called my brothers to tell them that Mom's situation was grave and that she was being moved to the ICU.

Unchanging Faith

The idea that my mother might not make it through the night seemed preposterous. But it started to sink in as a very real possibility. Back in the cubicle, we got Mama's pastor on the phone, who led us in prayer.

Mama hadn't said much up to this point but, as Pastor prepared to say "Amen," she quietly mouthed one of her favorite expressions: "My God is sufficient." Four words packed with meaning, grounded in faith. Words I had heard her repeat all my life.

This is what her mother had always believed, and this was what my mother believed. These are words she spoke in times of crisis and in times when she needed comfort. Her God was sufficient and would provide. For my mother, this fact was sacrosanct and unchangeable. Suddenly I felt a little shiver—maybe I wasn't so alone in this after all.

As we hung up with Pastor, I found the number of Roderic Pettigrew, the son of one of my father's dearest friends, and a soul so dear to all of my family. With a PhD from MIT and an MD in nuclear medicine, Rod is equal parts brains and compassion, the quintessential person to call in such times.

"Hang on, Glenda, don't do a thing. I'll be right back to you," said Rod. For the first time in several hours, I dared to breathe. Within fifteen minutes Rod was back on the phone as promised. He'd reached the head of neurology at Vanderbilt, who would be over within the hour.

I was relieved to find that the neurologist was a delightful doctor, kind and deliberate in his examination, clearly unbothered by the middle-of-the-night call so common in his profession.

He confirmed the diagnosis of a brain aneurysm and explained that Mama would require surgery. And soon. Complicating matters was the fact that the weakness was in a rare spot at the base of her brain— basically the top of the spine. This was a critical juncture, the source of nerves that regulate respiration and heartbeat. It all boiled down to a very necessary but very risky surgery. I started to wonder what could possibly be worse.

Mama sensed my anxiety (it was hard to miss at that point, although

I was desperately trying to hold it together). "Glenda, I don't want you to worry. Didn't you hear what I told the doctor? *My God is sufficient.*"

I answered, as I always have, "Yes, ma'am." And I tried to mean it.

My brothers had flown in and were there with us as we conferred early the next morning. We learned that there were two surgeons in the country considered the masters at this rare type of surgery. Ironically, one was back home in Atlanta at Emory University Hospital, but moving Mama at this point was out of the question. The second surgeon was right there at Vanderbilt. Hallelujah! A miracle appeared to be in the offing.

Within minutes that feeling of elation turned to despair. We learned that the Vanderbilt surgeon was set to leave on a family vacation. But as a courtesy to Rod, he left his home, where he was busy packing, and came to the hospital to confer with us about other possibilities.

Maybe because I was expecting something worse, it came right away. "I'm so sorry, Judge Hatchett, but I've promised my family this vacation for months. I just won't be able to do the surgery for your mom. But I feel very good recommending my colleague to you; I know he'll do an excellent job."

I was prepared to beg, and I did. If this guy was the best in the country, he was the one I wanted for Mama. Second best was just not going to cut it.

"Doctor," I implored one final time. "This is my mother…and, I mean, you just can't leave. You're the best, and how dare I not give her the very best?" He sat back down and, miraculously, agreed to try to postpone his vacation by a couple of days. Of course I understood what it means to keep promises to your kids. Clearly, this was our guardian angel on earth.

The neurosurgeon sent his family on and arranged to meet them a couple of days later. At this point the wheels of modern medicine moved into overdrive. Surgery would take place within hours. CT, MRI, blood tests, brain scans, you name it, they did it. When it came time to sign the consent form, Mama was adamant that she would sign the papers herself. She was not so incapacitated that she needed me or my brothers to sign for her. She took the paper—actually she sort of snatched it from my hand—and wrote her name in the same deliberate script we've always known.

I distinctly remember my mom's feistiness in this situation. No other patient in the ICU was conscious. No other patient was even talking. Yet my mother was alert and insisting that she could sign for her own procedures and be active in her own care.

When she was done, Mama looked up and handed me the pen—like the way the president signs a bill into law then hands the pen to someone who was instrumental in getting the legislation passed. As she did she repeated quietly, "My God is sufficient."

It was all she needed to say. Mama didn't need to know about the doctor's credentials, how many such surgeries he'd performed, or how the hospital scored on its last accreditation exam. The only information Mama needed was contained in those four words.

And that's why I share this story with you. Mama knew, even facing rare and risky brain surgery, that her God would ensure that tomorrow would be better than today. I think that for my mother, whether she woke up in heaven or woke up still with us, she would have viewed the glass as half full. She would have considered that a better day had dawned.

Facing an uncertain outcome, I was not so sure.

In final preparation for the surgery, a contrasting dye was run through Mama's arteries. This gives the doctor and his team one final image of the area that they will repair. It's like a road map that shows areas of construction and suggests necessary detours.

But here's where the story takes a totally unbelievable turn. After studying the results of the brain scan, the surgeon—who in less than a day had become our family's new best friend—strode into the room waving my mother's chart in his hand as he talked.

"Well, Mrs. Hatchett," he said to Mama, "I've got some very interesting news for you. Your aneurysm seems to have sealed itself." I gasped audibly. Mama was stone still. He sat down on the corner of the bed and continued.

"This is something neither I nor my colleagues have ever seen before!" This vessel that had been leaking blood had miraculously repaired. The veins had fused together, showing no sign of the former bulge that hours ago had been holding my mother's life hostage.

We stayed in Nashville a few days for the doctors to observe Mama and to verify the image that showed the repair. Back home we even checked back into Emory Hospital so that those fine doctors could corroborate the findings. Both groups considered this a medical miracle. In fact, one of the physicians had whispered to me as we left Vanderbilt that they had given her about a one in a hundred chance of surviving. But Mama had simply refused to doubt that a better outcome, a better day, was on the horizon.

Her God had, indeed, been sufficient.

Emotion and Health Are Related

My mother possesses the kind of faith and hope and optimism that we wish we could bottle. What if we could all heal ourselves, by believing that the outcome of every crisis will be good? If you or I could have this expectation on our shelves when we needed to add it to a recipe, we'd be able to cook up hope whenever we wanted.

Today, nearly fourteen years after this incident, Mama is going strong. She drives around town in her convertible, swims regularly, does endless good works, and thoroughly enjoys life, made strong by the faith that is her constant companion. Back in that hospital, Mama believed without a doubt that some way she would be healed, and that better days were ahead. But not all of us are blessed with her vision.

Difficulties are part of every life. We're called on to cope with horrible things—like the death of a child, a painful divorce, economic reversals, and so much more. How, in light of such sorrow, do we anticipate the best and, perhaps in focusing on the best, encourage a better outcome? It's not that wishing something makes it so. But expecting a positive outcome does make positive possibilities visible. Being optimistic does make positive strategies more clear. I believe that embracing a positive outcome opens us up to the possibilities that will bring it about.

I also believe that those of us who don't come by this thinking quite as naturally as my mother *can* train ourselves to become optimistic, to practice staying optimistic, and to use our positive expectation to make our lives more of what we need.

Not all of us will have the strength and power of vision that Clemmie Hatchett developed over decades. Her unwavering faith stands as a model of the power that comes with steady, unquestioning belief. All of us can practice this. All of us can learn to cultivate optimism. All of us can practice the important principle that emotion and health are related. We can learn the lesson that when we allow despair to take root in our lives, we make room for negativity and ill-health too.

Positivity and optimism are powers of vision. If we all practice seeing the good in our lives, then we open ourselves to much greater expressions of health, well-being, and promise.

Have there been times in your life when things seemed impossible to overcome? Were you told you had cancer, or was a loved one diagnosed with a serious illness? Do you need healing in your life today? Physical healing may require you to be more disciplined about your lifestyle and more positive about your outlook on life—are you willing? Maybe losing fifteen pounds would take the pressure off your aching joints? Emotional healing may be necessary. Are you carrying pain you suffered as a neglected child? Or are you enduring pain from debilitating or chronic depression? Perhaps today you need to heal from the pain of a bitter divorce? Are you trying to recover from devastating financial ruin? Have you been forced to acknowledge that you made wrong decisions and are you now paying the price?

Claim your healing now. Be tenacious knowing that each day you live brings new opportunities. Dare to take charge and dare to expect miraculous things to happen in your life. Believe in positive possibilities, even when life seems bleak.

Today:

Incorporate one specific thing into your lifestyle to support your best health. Write it down. Believe that you can live a healthy life and promise yourself today that you will do that specific one thing every day for the rest of your life in order to claim your best health (or your healing).

Dare To...

Be mindful about your physical and emotional health.

- Know that your good health depends on your positive and informed choices.
- Make the best decisions you can with your knowledge of your body, without unwarranted dependence on the advice of others.

Preserve and influence your health.

- Have faith in your ability to participate in your healing.
- Cultivate unshakable belief in your ability to have a healthy body and spirit.

Expect miracles and believe in the power of miracles, no matter what others who surround you are able (or unable) to expect or believe.

- Realize that your body and your spirit are both miraculously resilient.
- Know that your body and your emotions can heal and recover if you offer your gentle and consistent support.

Fifteen

You Define You

All of us are defined by our actions. This is true for every person in the world. We come to know ourselves by what we are able to motivate ourselves to do. People also come to know us by the actions we take. The importance of what we do cannot be overrated. If we dream, but fail to take action, we become disappointed in ourselves. If we take action, then our situation changes, our self-esteem increases, and we begin to feel more motivated to do more, to take next steps, to further our actions. Often, momentum will take over and help to keep us moving toward the goals we have set.

When we take action, others respond. Every action causes a reaction. And in spite of how people view us, or want to view us, our actions will dominate any given situation. Our actions are more powerful than our histories, than our words, than our names.

There are dozens, even hundreds of people any one of us can name whose actions have defined them and inspired us. Often, we remember and celebrate the actions people take in the midst of desperate

struggles. We have a long history, as a people, of victory through struggle. The actions we take in times of conflict help to make us who we
are. No matter who we become—hero, genius, mother, father, brother,
sister, inventor, thief—our actions are what make us known to others,
to our families, and to ourselves.

The Vivian Malone Story

When we do what we set out to do, we are able to reflect and say, "Yes,
I did it!" Recognizing what we've done—small action or big—defines
who we are to others, and also changes how we view ourselves. A good
friend of our family, Vivian Malone, was one of the many in our history
who changed her future, and our future as a nation, by her determination and steadfast action.

In 1963, as our nation struggled with the dream of equality and civil
rights for all Americans, the Malone family, along with a community of
friends and supporters, devised a plan of action. The state of Alabama
was ground zero for the civil rights movement. Efforts toward achieving this dream were met with violence by some citizens as well as
law enforcement. In spite of this resistance, desegregating the public
schools and providing all students with an equal opportunity to receive
a quality education remained a core goal of the civil rights movement.
The University of Alabama was and still remains the best and largest
public college in the state. If integration could be achieved there, it
could be achieved everywhere. The community and the Malone family
knew that they needed smart, courageous students to move this goal
to reality.

It should be noted that a great deal of behind-the-scene actions
were required before any African-American student could set foot on
the University of Alabama campus. One of the unsung heroes who

worked tirelessly toward achieving this dream was Attorney Fred Gray, a well-known civil rights lawyer from Tuskegee, Alabama. He spent many years of hard work and sleepless nights fighting the legal battle to obtain the necessary court order to force the integration of all public schools in Alabama, including the University of Alabama. With the court order and the U.S. Marshal's office in place, it was finally time to mount the steps of the university and change the daily practice of the segregated South.

On June 11, 1963, a warm summer morning dawned in Alabama, but the day got much hotter very quickly. "No niggers on campus! Go home, nigger bitch!" These taunts grew louder as Vivian Malone made her way up the steps to Foster Auditorium, on the University of Alabama campus. Vivian Malone and fellow African-American student James Hood, calling on their courage and tenacity, attempted to register for classes at the all-white University of Alabama.

The most formidable presence faced that day stood blocking the entrance to the building as the students approached. It was George Wallace, an avowed segregationist who was then governor of Alabama. Wallace had promised voters to end integration "at the schoolhouse door." He was attempting to make good on his public promise that morning, grandstanding in full view of the media and as the world watched. But those in the know believed that this was a battle George Wallace would not win.

With the entrance to the hall blocked, Vivian and James stepped into a nearby car to avoid the kind of physical brutality that racial conflict tended to breed in those years. They were only somewhat safer there. Bigots threw rocks at the windows. The standoff continued for more than four hours. After a pathetic last-ditch effort to challenge the constitutionality of the court order, Wallace finally turned away, relinquishing his thin hold on segregation in Alabama and forgoing his attempt to keep the students from entering. But for Malone and Hood, getting through the door was just the beginning.

Other battles for justice were under way elsewhere. On June 12, a day after the dramatic showdown at the university, civil rights leader Medgar Evers was gunned down in Johnson, Mississippi, by a Ku Klux Klansman. These legendary racist operatives fought the same battle as Wallace, but far outside the rule of law, and often in the secret dark of night.

The Ku Klux Klan was as publicly known and dreadfully feared as any organized group could be, but with hubris and cowardice combined, the members shrouded themselves in sheets, kept their faces and names from being known, and let their horrendous actions of calculated brutality speak volumes. The Klansmen's clearly identifiable hoods flaunted their presence. The whole nation watched. The work of the Klan was consistent, and was covered extensively in the media. Their atrocities were no secret. Only their identities were unknown. The men behind these masks and beneath these sheets did not stand up for their actions. They terrorized without revealing themselves, were often only identified years later, and in some instances were never identified at all.

Some Americans did protest, some resisted. State by state, racist "permissions" were dismantled. Segregation laws were challenged. Crime by crime, law by law, rule by rule, overt racist forces in America were confronted with the insistence that segregationists open the door to the future.

The air around the civil rights struggle was supercharged. There was a palpable fear of what the next day or week would bring—uncertainty about who would be beaten next, who might be shot, or who might go missing. I remember riding with my family down a local road, a two-lane highway heavily traveled by trucks. Dad was driving, Mom was in the front, and we three kids were in the back. When a rock flew up from a truck ahead of us and hit the windshield, my mother nearly leaped from her seat, certain that we had been shot at. That's the way things felt.

Of course, we never traveled at night in those days. Any shrouded menace might be lurking in the darkness. We would leave at daybreak, always certain of the motels where blacks were welcome, or we set out having been invited ahead of time to stay with friends or relatives along the way. We were vulnerable and often felt afraid.

This was the atmosphere of threat, violence, and hatred in which Vivian and James finally registered for class. They ate their meals alone, either mocked or ignored by the school's white student body.

In later years, Vivian would recall smiling at fellow students as she walked to class, though no smiles were ever offered in return. Once she dared to say "good morning" and was spat upon for her courtesy. In Mobile, her family needed police protection in order to be safe in their home. In those times, of course, you could not really know who on the police force you could trust, because some policemen in the Deep South were also Klansmen. In order to supplement the "police protection," the men in Vivian's family took turns standing guard so that they could be awake and alert to protect the family.

The cruelty and isolation proved overwhelming for James Hood, who left very shortly after that fateful morning. Vivian was left to integrate the University of Alabama alone. Hood was not the first African-American student to have been run off by the racist climate at UA. In 1956, Autherine Lucy, from Shiloh, Alabama, attended UA after being admitted to a graduate program in teaching. Sources report that Lucy was run off the campus by angry mobs, and was "expelled" one month after leaving. The battle against segregation in education was being fought on many fronts, and by individuals both known and anonymous.

Despite verbal threats, bomb threats, and painful isolation, Vivian soldiered on. Within two years, she became the first African-American student to graduate from the University of Alabama, the university she integrated. Vivian earned a degree in business management and went on to work for the Civil Rights Division of the U.S. Department of Justice. I've tried, but it's nearly impossible for me to imagine the atmosphere she endured. The "fun" college experience we've come to expect of our first forays into independence were a foreign shore for Vivian, who studied on the front line. She undoubtedly experienced tension 24/7—a sense of never being able to let her guard down, never a moment of peace. Add to this her worry of knowing that her family was being targeted back home. The entire Malone family played a role in the righteous fight for justice.

I am appalled even today when considering this organized and relentless inhumanity. Spitting on a college student who says good morning is nothing short of pathological. I can't imagine being chased off a campus by a howling, angry mob. In an age of mass media and open sightings, a full one hundred years after slavery, a high-achieving African-American student could not expect to safely study, could not expect to expand her mind. This is part of the shameful legacy of our country. This is modern history. This is the baseline for the triumph of Vivian Malone, and others like her.

Vivian taught me three important lessons. First, one person, with the love and support of others, can change the landscape. Although two students began the struggle to integrate the University of Alabama, after that first victory Vivian had to study at the university alone. She had no community of other African-American students with whom to share the experience, from whom to gather strength. I can't imagine how lonely, and maybe frightened, Vivian Malone must have been. But history has proved that she endured and triumphed. The unnamed custodians, housekeepers, and others who worked on the campus of the University of Alabama knew and shared her dream and showed great kindness toward her during those very difficult years. The community and the Malone family stood behind her every step of the way, but without her courage and commitment to bring the dream to reality, the civil rights movement might have taken a very different course.

Second, Vivian Malone taught me that it is not what you are called but rather what name you choose to answer to. You can deflect the power of being called names by refusing to answer to insults and slurs. Years after coming to understand her example, I continued to see the deep importance of this lesson.

Third, achieving dreams is not easy work! Achievement takes work on all fronts: dreaming, aiming, dedication, and *daily action*. Remember, dreams are realities every day! Vivian Malone proved that if you dare, you can make a difference; you can reach beyond the limits set by others.

In 1963, Governor George Wallace had considerable political and popular support for his racist views. In direct defiance of the law, Wallace tried to deny students entry into the building, and to deny them higher education at the state university. Decades later, Wallace apologized for his actions and sought reconciliation with Vivian, calling her "a true American hero."

Many believe he knew the game was up on June 11 but chose to posture for the media and for his supporters. At one point, Deputy Attorney General Nicholas Katzenbach said, "From the outset, Governor, all of us have known that the final chapter of this history will be the admission of these students."

Evil bows to the pressures of time and to the insistent demands for justice coming from our people and our allies. We gained social victories, but individuals like Vivian fought those battles that changed opportunity and possibility for us all.

In the ordinary effort to go from childhood to adulthood, to attend college and prepare for work, Vivian Malone had to do what none had done before her. Vivian marched on heroically. Her legacy of courage and conviction changed the landscape for all of us, people of all races. Her name should be known, sung, remembered.

It's Not What You're Called, but What You Answer To

When I was a young girl, in Georgia, I had a bad experience at a store. I was with my mother, shopping, and some boys called as I passed them in the parking lot, something about a "nigger." At the time, I was instantly outraged. In a rush of fury, I said to my mother, "Did you hear them? Did you hear what they called me?" My mother insisted that nobody called me a nigger. I insisted that they did, and at the same time I knew she had to have heard them. My mother repeated, firmly, that nobody had called me a nigger. My mother insisted because she was trying to teach me that if I did not acknowledge people's ignorance and insults, it was the same as if their insults did not exist. If we refuse to give our attention to insults, then insults lose their power to injure us.

Every child learns the singsong adage, "Sticks and stones may break my bones, but words will never hurt me." The strategy of *rejecting* what people call you, however, is more active than that. As we enter into adult relationships and build intimacy, what people call us does matter, especially the people we trust and depend on. If a partner or husband or wife or colleague or boss or best friend calls you names, pronounces you worthless, defective, or unintelligent, the vile language and maddening behavior can influence you without your realizing.

In my courtroom, I faced many people who, in times of trial, insulted and verbally abused others. Particularly for women, domestic issues would arise that caused me to wonder, and sometimes to ask, why a woman would remain in a household or a relationship with a man who insulted her or verbally abused her. To my chagrin and surprise, many of the women who were confronted with this problem seemed to either believe or accept the insults they were charged with!

Really, I can't count how many times I encounter women who are called "no good," and who don't seem to react indignantly or with outrage. When I ask, "Why stay with a person who's abusive or horrible?" women admit to believing no one else will have them. They acknowledge not wanting to spend their lives alone.

And this is where the lesson Vivian Malone and my mother taught applies. Just because someone calls you a name, just because someone calls you worthless, or unattractive, or curses you in any way, does *not* mean you have to answer to what they call you. If you do respond to epithets and insults, you run the risk of becoming accustomed to opinions of you that are negative and inappropriate.

What you think of yourself is what matters in this life. If you allow others to hurl insults at you, *and you answer to them*, then you do yourself the disservice of allowing their poisonous thoughts to enter into your consciousness. Just like any idea—or germ or virus—without resistance against negativity, the names you answer to can take root in your soul.

Unfortunately, I see this as a dangerous pattern for women who are frightened of being alone. Abuse and insults, however, are not worth answering to. This kind of poison is no poison to choose.

You are in charge of defining yourself. You are in charge of what names you answer to.

I encourage you to realize that if you face any situations where others insult you or verbally abuse you, take the first step, and *don't answer.*

It's not what you're called but what you answer to that will define who you are. Anyone can call you any name in the book, but if you are determined to define yourself for yourself, you must make them wonder who they think they're talking to. Be strong. Show them that they *certainly* can't be talking to you. Refuse to answer. It's what you answer to that defines you.

Vivian Malone was called many horrible names by angry people who wanted her stopped. But she just kept walking. She never stopped—or stooped—to answer. Vivian Malone had serious business to take care of; she had a university, a state, and a nation to change.

Nobody who insults you wants to talk to you anyway. People who insult you and call you names want to trip you up. Insults are designed to make you fail, to make you doubt yourself. Don't. Do not give people who hurl epithets at you the power to get in your way or to diminish your self-concept. Keep believing in who you are. Moving forward with faith and belief *in yourself* is the only way to thrive in this life.

I knew Vivian, and felt inspired by her, until her death in 2005. I never once saw her bitter. Instead she operated from a place of deep faith and firm insistence. When you could get her to talk about her historic role, which was not often, Vivian said she simply did what she had to do. As she walked those stairs she did not focus on the names she was being called, but focused instead on *what she was being called to do.* What a brilliant summation of nation-stopping work. Clearly it would have been so easy to get distracted or dispirited, but she did not. Clearly it would have been permissible and understandable for her to trumpet her accomplishment, but she did not.

Of the many amazing people who have blessed my life, Vivian was and still is my quintessential role model—her walk of faith, her dedication to her husband and family, and her resolve in the face of illness. I got to know Vivian personally; her family and our family became like kin to each other.

On the day of her funeral, October 19, 2005, Nicholas Katzenbach, Atlanta Mayor Shirley Franklin, and Eric Holder were among those offering tributes. So many people who mattered to the national landscape attended; so many people showed they cared. Vivian's dear family asked me to speak, a request that humbled me to the core. I tried to stand for Vivian. I crafted my words and maintained my posture in order to try to do justice to all Vivian Malone had been. I prayed that I could speak clearly and honorably to the thousands of mourners who crowded the Martin Luther King Chapel at Morehouse. Others spoke before me, telling beautiful stories of her courageous life and what she meant to them and to our nation.

When my turn came, I thanked the family for the privilege of paying honor to my longtime friend. I told the audience how I had looked up to Vivian, my role model who had it all—class, brains, and boundless faith. I spoke of how Vivian stood "knocking" on that door in 1963, so that I and my children and generations unborn would never have to knock again. The courage it took to stand in the midst of that hatred and keep knocking on that door is amazing to think of even today. I couldn't help knocking on the pulpit as I spoke.

Vivian, I explained to the congregation of mourners, knew the source of her own strength, and knew the sound and strength of her own name. She would not be diminished by the hatred of the Klan, by segregationists, or by folk who were just plain ignorant.

For those who did not remember, I painted a picture of the standoff and Foster Auditorium. *"On one side stood those dedicated to preserving a segregated South. They called her names, spewing hatred with their speech. Had George Wallace asked any of us in this room, we certainly would have told him to save the trouble—you don't bet against a winner! Not only was Vivian Malone a winner that day when she stood up to Wallace and his boys, she is and will be a winner through all eternity."*

Before dawn on the Thursday morning when she transitioned from labor to reward, she stood at the ultimate door. *"Now,"* I said as I nodded to the venerable Nicholas Katzenbach, *"Vivian did not need you. She did not need any of us. Vivian walked serenely and faithfully alone, as she approached heaven's gates. There was no crowd of haters spitting and cursing at her. No, my friends, instead there was a sweet choir of angels cheering for her, bidding her closer.*

"Imagine with me how her steps quickened as she approached. See her run toward the gate. See the singing angels accompanied by the sweet sounds of Gabriel and his boys on the trumpets. She needed no petition. Vivian Malone did not need a court order. Not this time.

"Vivian arrived, and the Heavenly Father flung open wide heaven's gate. He said, 'Welcome home, Vivian. You've run the good race. You fought the good fight. You persevered until the end. Welcome, my dear and faithful servant. Welcome home, welcome home.'"

The congregation rose to its feet, but they were not standing and shouting for me. They were filling the room with love and applause for Vivian. I was so grateful to God to have been able to deliver the words that reflected what was in my heart.

The first Mother's Day after Vivian passed I spent with Vivian's daughter Monica, a new mother. This baby was the grandchild Vivian never knew. It was a sad and sweet time we will remember forever. Vivian's absence left a hole in the room and a hole in our hearts, but having had her in our lives was a tremendous joy.

When faced with injustice, what do you do? When you see a friend or stranger mistreated, do you stand up for right? Do you answer to the voice of good? Do you ignore or silence the competing negative sounds?

Perhaps you hesitated to apply for a promotion because someone had called you unable, and you chose to answer to that rather than what you know is true about you? Can you call yourself confident, competent, and ready to succeed, or do the names others call you drown out your own voice? What name do you answer to, what agenda do you follow? How do these influence the actions you take?

Vivian Malone knew what and whom to answer to. She answered to her good name, and she answered to her righteous intentions. Because of her refusal to answer to slurs, or to fear, or to distractions, she made progress that benefits every one of us. Because of her steadfast action, her name came to stand for courage and faith.

Every one of us can make a name for ourselves—but only by our actions. Nothing but action can define us.

Be absolutely certain that the way you define yourself informs how you go about living your life. Are you a strong person? Then live strong. Are you a smart person? Then engage in smart activities. Are you a loving person? Then do not allow your expressions of love to lapse.

Today:

Decide that from this day forward only you will define you. Make a firm choice to never let anyone else define who you are or what you believe. Take twenty seconds now to quickly write down seven words that best define you. You may be surprised by what you learn from making this list.

Dare To...

Do what you are called to do.

- Take the time to assess how you feel called.
- Have faith in what you can accomplish.

Fight the good fight.

- Mobilize yourself—and your family and your friends—for what you know is right.
- Consider the "battles" you are engaged in and make sure they are worthy of your energy.

Choose new battles.

- Define what you will be known for working toward.
- Use your power for the good you see needs creating in our world.

Sixteen

Lifting As We Climb

Lessons come to us when we need to learn them. And any lesson we don't learn keeps coming back until we do. The lesson that our lives, our blessings, and our good fortune are meant to be shared comes to most of us in childhood. We look at our children in the same way that teachers and other guardians do, in the same way that we were looked at when we were growing up: Does she play well with others? Does he share his toys? Will she divide the cookies? Will he offer his sister some of his popcorn? If we could not or would not, as children, demonstrate that we could share, then what happened? We weren't allowed to have whatever kept us selfish. This lesson is ultra-important. Our blessings are meant to be shared.

A Teachable Moment

I remember learning a big lesson early about my failure to share. I was young, it was Easter, and I didn't want to share with Rhonda Bell.

The Bells were a couple who were such close friends of our family that we children called them Auntie and Uncle. We knew them all our lives. Auntie and Uncle Bell both taught high school French. Their ability to speak this exotic and beautiful language was one of the many things about them that fascinated and impressed me. And of course, they did not hesitate to *parlez français* when they didn't want us kids to understand what they were discussing.

Childless themselves, they doted on my brothers and me, and we enjoyed their attention. One summer, their niece, Rhonda, came to live with them. I was about nine, and Rhonda was close to my age. I had a new friend, and we two spent wonderful summertimes being girls and playing. To this day, I don't know what the circumstances were that brought Rhonda, though after being a judge, I can imagine some possibilities.

My mother was a skilled seamstress, and she made many of my clothes by hand. This kept my mother in greater control of her daughter's dress and our family finances than we could ever imagine today. I had a closet full of handmade clothes so beautiful that sometimes, after my pristine outfits got too small, I would convince Mama to let me hold on to them a little longer before giving them to other, smaller children, to see if I could get just one more wear.

Each year, my mother and I went on our Easter shopping trip, just us two, to find fabric for my new Easter dress. This annual ritual was always a special treat for me. The spring after Rhonda came, she and Auntie Bell went along. I minded sharing, but just a little. I was still a child, and as much as my parents modeled good behavior, I still had some resistance to sharing my mother's time.

But the promise of the day calmed me down: a new Easter dress, the joy of choosing from all the new spring colors, and the treat of Dairy Queen after shopping.

We spent plenty of time in the fabric aisles, fingering and rejecting seersuckers, taffetas, and ginghams. That year, Mama and I settled on a beautiful yellow eyelet with white underlay. Mama picked out the perfect matching lace. Rhonda chose a blue-and-orange fabric that I did not think was very pretty. But to each her own.

My mother and I carefully selected a delicate lace trim that would make the edges of my outfit extra special. We bought dress material from the bolts of fabric, and just a little of the expensive, darling lace. At the end of the trip, our ice cream was delicious, and the four of us had a good time.

One night, after I had gone to bed, I heard the comforting hum of my mother sewing in the next room. I was not asleep, and I decided to go in and get a peek at my mother's sewing. Sitting at the sewing machine, my mother was finishing up Rhonda's blue-and-orange dress, but Mother was adding *my* precious lace to Rhonda's dress.

"Mama, what are you doing with *my lace*?" I actually stomped my foot and had a little tantrum—which was not tolerated in our house. My mother sat back and stared at me, and then responded coolly, "I think you recognize this fabric, Glenda. What I am doing is making an Easter dress for a little girl who doesn't have a mother."

Not having a mother was a new idea for me. All my friends had mothers. Although I loved and appreciated my mother, I had never thought of not having her.

I knew I was wrong. I perfectly remember the sad, sickish feeling that came over me. My heart sank and my eyes filled with tears. There I stood in my robe and slippers, embarrassed and deflated, showing my mother I did not know how to behave. I was better trained than my behavior showed.

Despite everything I deserved, Mama did not raise her voice at me. She didn't call me out for acting like a spoiled brat. She didn't punish me or threaten to tell Daddy what I'd done (although I'm sure she did, as soon as he came home). Instead, Mama reached for me. She just reached for me. She pulled me close, and I instinctively put my head to her chest, where we remained for a long, wordless moment.

The air was filled with so much Mama did not say. She did not choose to remind me how much I had in my life compared to so many. She did not tell me that giving is a blessing and that we only grow by lifting others along with us as we climb.

God's great measure of mercy enters our lives when we are not only undeserving, but when we are *least* deserving. That's exactly what happened that moment as I stood in the sewing room, fuming and raging.

God's mercy worked through my mother, turning my selfishness into a tender, teachable moment neither of us would ever forget. Mama used the experience to teach me about the value of caring about somebody other than myself.

I appreciated my mother, and said thank you for all she did for me— and had always been sincere with my expressions of gratitude. I had a wonderful mother who was there for me every day, on good and not-so-good days, to love me, to take care of me, encourage me, and teach me right from wrong. What would my life feel like if, one day, she was not there? I had a mother whom I could touch, and who could touch me, and who touched my soul. I had something Rhonda would never have no matter how many beautiful dresses were lined up in her closet. And no matter how much Mama shared herself with others (something she continues to do to this day), there would always be enough for me. How dare I begrudge Rhonda what my mother selflessly offered?

In retrospect, I would not have considered myself an overly selfish child, and probably wasn't. It felt good to share my dolls and books with Rhonda. But with the Easter dress, the shopping trip, the precious lace—things got a little too close for comfort. When Rhonda was given something special, something only I had, something that went beyond everyday use, I no longer wanted to share. Of course, I needed to learn a lesson. The pain and shame I felt that day were difficult but necessary teachers.

It's never too late to make a difference, and it's never too early. We are all interdependent. We inspire others by our actions, and by our example. And we devalue ourselves and our communities when we are selfish and do not help. Rhonda Bell and I both had a more memorable Easter, both of us wearing dresses lovingly sewn by my mother, and Rhonda's dress was decorated with my lace. Rhonda chose what she wanted, and I chose for myself. And my mother, who orchestrated a holiday we will *both* always remember, taught me an enormous lesson—that the nature of life is to share.

Debt of Gratitude

Over the years I've learned words to accompany the feelings I experienced as a child. One expression I often use (and it's hardly original) is, "Blessings are not ours to keep." In fact, blessings are intended to flow through us, if we are open to them. Blessings are meant to go forward and bless the world. The concept of multiplying good deeds is as old as faith itself.

To respond to a debt of gratitude by spreading our blessings has the tremendous potential to change and improve our families and communities. Every one of us is in turn able to offer what we are given.

Not long ago, the popular movie *Pay It Forward*, based on a book of the same name by Catherine Ryan Hyde, reignited this important practice. The book and the movie told the story of *creating* a kindness to offer to others, as a result of some kindness being offered to you.

In response to a school assignment, twelve-year-old Trevor McKinney comes up with a unique idea that he turns into an action plan. He'll do a good deed for someone. In turn, Trevor asks that person to perform an act of kindness for three other people. He wants each of those people, performing their own individual acts of generosity, to each ask the three others to do the same. All kinds of new events and unexpected changes happen for Trevor and the people he loves as a result of his big idea. Their world really does change for the better.

My life has been blessed beyond measure by so many. Attempting to return the goodness—to them or to the world—helps keep me properly grounded. Everyone depends on someone, sometime, for something; we all need to recognize this, and be dependable in turn. And in Hyde's wonderful way of expressing this idea, we ideally pay forward, using our blessings, our intelligence, and our energy to help others.

I love the idea of paying forward. I've always believed in finding meaningful ways to acknowledge the debts I owe to others, even if the kind words or deeds were *gifts*. An important part of feeling gratitude in your life, and being able to see what you have to be thankful for, is to be stronger about your courtesy. When we say thank you, we can say thank you *actively*.

Here's a good example. When my first son was born, I was in the typical new-mom tizzy—excited, sleepless, and somewhat clueless about my new role as mother.

One afternoon when my son was just a couple of weeks old the doorbell rang. Gillian, a beautiful Jamaican woman who lived around the corner, stood at the door, smiling, as she juggled bowls and packages and her one-year-old Lauren on her hip. I made way for her to enter, not exactly sure what she had in mind, but pleased to see an adult for any reason.

Gillian dumped everything in the kitchen, handed her daughter to me, and returned to the car to get a portable playpen and a couple of grocery bags. "Glenda, it's your lucky day. Lauren and I are here to help. Go on upstairs—you look like you could use a nap. The kids and I are going to have some playtime, then we're going to make you dinner."

I was speechless; it was such a welcome surprise. What I didn't know then was that the first weeks of parenthood are universally overwhelming. Anyone who has been there knows what it's like: barely any sleep, hair undone, and in your nightgown until noon. Gillian, an "old hand" at parenting, knew exactly what I needed. I complied and walked upstairs, fell immediately into a deep sleep, and woke two hours later to the smell of something good cooking and Gillian singing to the babies!

I got up, nursed my son, and looked around the house. It was as if a fairy had flown in—laundry was done and folded, the kitchen and family room were picked up, and dinner was made. There was a wonderful sense of domestic peace. No matter how long it's been, you parents can probably relate. Those first weeks are a time of such focused concentration on the new baby that you just can't seem to get anything else done. When it does get done, it feels like a miracle!

Gillian, clearly a gracious person, could have dropped off a casserole or a baby gift and I would have been delighted. But as she later explained to me, a cousin had done something similar when Lauren was a newborn. Gillian vowed that she would return the favor by reaching out to another new mom, and did she ever! And how glad was I to be the recipient! That one afternoon of pampering and rest gave me a real mental and physical boost. After years, the grace and sincere caring shown by my neighbor still burns bright in my memory and in my heart.

Over the years, I have treated other new moms to a similar gift of tender, loving care.

Finding a way to repay kind offerings is key to the idea of paying forward. In order to change our lives for the better, we are much better off if we become creative about what we do. Each of us thinks like no other person. Each of us is gifted with the heart and mind we have. When we connect with our God-given minds and hearts, our uniqueness shines through. We behave like no other person in the universe, because each of us is one of a kind.

So if we would first acknowledge what we've been given, by God and by other people in our lives, and then *decide* how we are going to express our gratitude—how we're going to pay forward—then what we've done is made our devotions personal. We have connected what we feel with what we do. This connection—between emotion and action—is truly the core of personality, and builds self-esteem. Believe me, the more we define our own responses in this life, the more we take action based on what we've defined for ourselves, the better we feel, and the more our lives reflect who we are.

Daring to be who we are changes lives. Daring to create ways to give changes families and communities. Being only what the day, or the boss, or inactive living will allow only permits us to survive. We all know that surviving is necessary, but also insufficient. We want to thrive! Thriving is an *active* word.

A Gift and a Duty

At my church, the Mothers Board is a group of esteemed elder women appointed by the pastor, who hold a special place in the life of our congregation. At the Providence Missionary Baptist Church, which the Hatchett family has attended since my parents were married, members of the Mothers Board wear white, including hats and gloves, every Sunday. Even in August—when any extra bit of clothing adds measurable discomfort to the hot, motionless air of late summer in Atlanta—the Mothers Board assembles in their regalia and sits as a watchful presence.

The Mothers have a place of honor across from the deacons, in pews running perpendicular to those of the rest of the congregation. During services most of the congregation sees them in profile. In my child's eye, this made the Mothers seem even more dignified and important. Their duties were firmly established and included preparing the communion table with freshly laundered linens and their devotion.

Among the mothers then were Mother Duncan, Mother Allen, Mother Whatley, Mother Berry, Mother Echols, Mother Jordan, Mother Hicks, Mother Kelly, and Mother Gomillian. They made a point to greet every one of us. I imagine that they privately noted who was absent on any given Sunday.

The weekend before I was to leave home for Mount Holyoke College was busy with last-minute shopping, packing, and goodbyes. Heading off to college was a very big deal, but not big enough to warrant missing church.

After services, we all mingled in the sanctuary for a few minutes before going home to Sunday dinner. Mother Odessa Duncan came up to me. Everyone knew everyone else in our church, so even though Mother Duncan was not part of my parents' close circle, it was not surprising that she would know I was about to leave for school. I figured she would offer a hug and good wishes.

But Mother Duncan had something else in mind. Smiling, she reached for my right hand, pulling me toward her. She placed a little wrapped bundle in my palm—a white handkerchief embroidered with a delicate red rose. Into each corner of the hanky, Mother Duncan had painstakingly tied a silver half dollar.

As I looked up at her, she folded my fingers around the packet and took both of my hands in hers. "Baby," she said, "I want you to run on. I can't go where you're going, but you run on, baby." Then she hugged me and, before I could barely utter a thank-you, turned and walked away.

I clutched the little bundle until we got home, where I opened it and reflected on the simple yet deeply significant and beautiful gesture.

I do not believe Mother Duncan finished high school, and I have no idea at what point her formal education may have ended and for what reasons. But I was certain of one thing: Mother Odessa Duncan had never seen the inside of a college campus and could only dream of the possibilities on my doorstep.

What was important is that one of her own—a child of the church—was heading off for experiences this wise woman knew would be life-changing. Mother Duncan did not raise me, but, like so many folks at church, she raised me up. She was part of a community whose members cared for each other in ways large and small.

From cooking in times of celebration to offering comfort in times of mourning, from baptisms and communions and holidays to lost jobs and new babies, life-cycle events were shared in this wonderful congregation that was my family.

The packet Mother Duncan lovingly pressed on me, four silver half dollars, amounted to two dollars. But her gift had real value that could never be calculated or fully measured. That modest yet magnificent gift symbolized all I'd been given, taught, and entrusted with. Mother Duncan's carefully prepared offering was a symbol of her hope and expectation, her caring and pride.

When Mother Duncan told me to "run on," she wasn't just wishing me good luck or urging me do well in school. She was telling me to embrace the opportunities before me and do what I needed to bring honor to myself and my community. Her charge to me to "run on" contained wisdom, sacrifice, and hope for me and generations yet born. In a poetic sense, she was telling me to run on ahead to higher ground, to a place that she could not go. Mother Duncan was telling me there was much work to be done—passing the baton to me in a kind of generational relay. She couldn't run this leg of the race with me. It was mine to run.

Knowing I had not gotten to Mount Holyoke by myself carried a huge responsibility, much bigger than any I'd face in Western Civ or Intro to Psychology. Mother Duncan's coins represented wealth beyond measure, and an expectation that I would find ways to return the caring, the generosity, and the heartfelt encouragement.

The four half dollars and Mother Duncan's words assured me that I was not going to college alone. Though she would never see the world that I was entering, Mother Duncan and all the Mothers would be spiritually by my side as I grew and attempted to create a life of purpose. So would my parents, the deacons, my godparents, my aunts and uncles, and so many generations who went before.

I stand on the shoulders of generations past. My path was made possible by those who pressed on through incredible hardship—through slavery, segregation, quotas, and the more subtle forms of discrimination that persisted decades after the laws had been changed.

I stand on the shoulders of those who stood boldly in the face of indignity and inhumanity. Who made their way through lynchings and beatings when hope seemed hopeless and change was barely a dream.

They raised me up and invested in me, and now I would have to *find a way* to repay the debt. Engaging my creativity and my personality as I define how to honor the gifts given to me—this is how "blessings flow through" me. None of us is much helped by receiving and not giving. We may benefit temporarily, but eventually we become "bloated" spiritually. Giving *and* receiving go hand in hand. Accepting and sharing are a part of one cycle, really. We have to give in order to receive. When we receive, we have to give in order to make room for new blessings to appear and take shape.

The generations who came before me, who made my achievement

possible, set the greatest example for paying a debt forward. I do everything I can, in the spirit of Mother Duncan, to not just offer money, or symbols, or prayer, or good wishes. I try to actively engage with college students in my life, to pay the debt of generations forward. To offer to others the spirit of support and hopefulness and generosity and expectation—because all these helped me make my way.

Making a Real *Difference*

The practice and the consistent expectation that we "give back," that we make a contribution to our community and our society, creates a structure for us to keep our values in play. This is so important for us—children and adults alike. What good is it to *believe* in helping if you don't help in a practical way? What does it mean to "love your neighbor" if you don't know your neighbors? What sense does it make to expect our children to "help those who are less fortunate" if they have never been in the same room with a foster child or a homeless person or if they've never seen the inside of a shelter?

For many of us, especially the young among us, our values exist, but we have yet to nurture them to take root and grow strong. Our values need outlets, practice, and repetition through action to develop.

I remember waking one morning at my parents' house and literally tripping over blankets and bodies in our living room in Atlanta. I was still a very young child. Civil rights activists were working, protesting, and sacrificing to nurture new values in the American South. My parents had decided to house a group of freedom riders—college students challenging the segregated buses, trains, and lunch counters throughout the Deep South. There were no advance plans for the freedom riders to come to our house, but our hosting them was important and typical of the service that was part of our family's life. We were raised to find ways to help. This idea bears repeating. Our contribution to our community required that we do more than help; we had to figure out *how* to help. This practice of creative action has had a major impact on my ability to do the work I do now. *Finding ways to help* is *the work I do now.*

My parents were always reaching out. They set an amazing example for me and my brothers. My mother refinished furniture for a family that had been burned out. My father rebuilt a playground at the local Y. I remember being about thirteen, an age when weekends were all about friends. But Mama insisted I spend time helping her strip and refinish furniture so that people in need in our community could reuse the good furniture instead of dealing with worn, low-quality dressers and chairs. Every day I watched my mother pack extra lunches to take to the school where she taught, so that no child went without a sandwich. My parents were careful observers, paying attention to where there were needs in our community and doing the best they could to help. Their commitment to service has taken root in me and followed me through life.

A birth or a death in our close-knit Atlanta neighborhood sent Mama and other neighborhood women into a predictable whirlwind of cooking. Hams and turkeys and rich chocolate cakes and salty greens and slow-cooked beans fueled celebrations and comforted mourners. In our intimate community, an unfamiliar face at church warranted an invitation to Sunday dinner. When newcomers moved in, Daddy would spend the weekend helping plant shrubbery and grass seed while Mama cultivated the new friendship with one of her signature desserts—a peach cobbler or lemon meringue pie. These days, more often than not, desserts are chosen from frozen food aisles, and our relationships have become more wary and less warm.

For Mom and Dad, there was plenty of organized outreach. Every

Easter our church hosted children in foster care from the Carrie Steele–Pitts Home. Mother and Godmother Irene would delight in providing a holiday experience these children could never have dreamed of. Dad chaired the local YMCA and lent his hand and wisdom to so many good causes. Giving back was all around, an active part of life.

I realize that for many people reaching out is difficult, or just unfamiliar. Life is more complicated than ever, and for most of us, taking care of ourselves and our families is about all we can handle. For people without role models in service, like my parents, to try may feel daunting. But even when coping with the day-to-day challenges of being human, sharing one's blessings is a wonderful strategy. Giving what we have to give serves us *and* serves others.

At the end of the day it simply is not enough for me—or for any of us—to be flourishing while others are suffering. To be concerned about others and reach beyond our comfort zone may not be easy. But outreach is more than necessary in this game of life. The challenge is to identify outreach that is both meaningful and possible for you.

If some of us are not all right, then our communities are not all right. It's not enough to retreat—behind a gated community or behind difficult personal challenges—and ignore the troubles of others. That belief has influenced my work as a judge and as a human being. We are all trying to thrive in this world, and we should help others to thrive as well.

To tell the truth, "giving back" has saved many an American community, or ethnic group, or individual in need. And isn't it true that every child—dependent as they are on us adults—is a child in need? How many of us feel fear and horror to think of our children lost, or unsupervised, or otherwise unattended to? Every one of us who has a child depends on somebody—teacher, pastor, neighbor, babysitter, school principal—to watch over our child until we can get there. We all run late, have accidents, depend on others' kindnesses every once in a while.

The key, though, is to not limit our giving to once in a while. The values we teach and that we believe in need to consistently extend out into our world. We are all blessed, and we all have something we can do or give.

We casually consider that people who are successful give *because* they have "arrived." But the truth is, a lot of the discipline and devotion and foresight and hard work that contributes to making us successful is developed *as we find ways to give.*

The Nature of Life Is to Share

All of life is a cycle. What we give—time, talents, resources—comes back to us in turn. We give and we receive. We sow and we reap. We find ways to contribute to others, and we put ourselves on the path of contributions that benefit us.

When I was invited to speak at the Morehouse Freshman Convocation, I issued a similar challenge. "Look around," I said to the new and excited students. "Take a good look, because there is someone who should be in this room today who isn't. Somebody who's back home in Oakland, Chicago, or rural Mississippi. I want you to find that person, figure out what kept them from success, and help them achieve it. Because it's not enough for you to be a Morehouse man. You have to lift others up as you climb, and it starts today."

When I speak to high school groups, I often end by asking, "Who among you are honor students?" Several raise their hands. Then I say, "I'd like to challenge you to identify someone who's not an honor student and reach out to that person. Become his or her cheerleader, tutor, mentor, friend, whatever it takes to lift them up. Because it's not enough for you to be on the honor roll if there's an opportunity to reach out and bring someone else along with you."

Then I expand the idea and suggest this to my young listeners. "If academics isn't your gift, what is? Can you sing beautifully? Are you a musician? If so, grab a few friends and volunteer to organize a kids' choir. Are you an athlete? Sign on to coach a youth sports league."

After I ask a number of questions, I suggest multiple possibilities for giving back. Then, finally, I always ask, "If you don't have a gift you think you could share, please stand up." *And no one ever stands.*

Find ways to help in your own community, share your particular talents. Decide what you will offer and contribute. Look at your talents and your resources—consider your blessings and resolve now to share them.

Maybe it is spending one hour a week on your way home from work reading to the elderly at a nursing home or visiting with an elderly gentleman who has no family that spends time with him. Perhaps it is coaching little league soccer—after all, you were a pretty good player in high school. Perhaps you staff a phone bank to help raise money for a worthy cause. Perhaps you volunteer one Saturday each quarter to help build a Habitat for Humanity house, or work as a CASA volunteer to help children in foster care, or volunteer at your local Boys and Girls Club. Perhaps you write a check to fund music lessons for a child whose parents do not have a checkbook. Perhaps you are a talented writer and you volunteer to write grant proposals and press releases for your favorite charity. Or maybe tonight you begin by cleaning out the closets in your home and donating items to a family in need. Maybe today you simply begin by doing one thing for someone else.

Your house of worship, your workplace, and your community are filled with opportunities. Whatever service you elect to offer, whatever value or life principle your service reinforces, it's important to contrib-ute, and to model this truth: *Service is the rent we pay for the privilege of living on this earth.* My friend Robert Allen raises the question: Are you current on your rent? It's never too early to inspire others by your example, or to help others with your efforts. It's never too late to begin.

Remember, your blessings flow *through* you to in turn bless the world.

Today:

For a just a moment, reflect upon your many blessings. Decide to do just one specific thing for someone else today, to make his or her life a little better. Once you've spread a blessing, make a note in your Joy Journal describing the experience. Did the experience of doing something for someone else give you joy? Might you be encouraged to do something specific for someone else again tomorrow, and the day after, and the day after that...?

Dare To...

Become a careful observer.

- Pay attention to needs in the communities where you live and work.
- Get involved, possibly even in communities you only pass through.
- Do the best you can to help.

Accept this important truth: you can make a difference.

- Start where you are with what you have.
- Create a way to share blessings you feel grateful for with others.
- Find a practical way to pass your blessings through you.

Discover how you can help better our world.

- Think more widely than the small circumference you travel on a daily basis.
- Make your life larger by applying your energies and efforts to problems that interest you.
- Extend your vision and your efforts beyond your family and your work life.

Seventeen

Write Your Own Story

We learn so much as children that never leaves our conscious minds. Plato wrote tens of centuries ago, "The beginning is the most important part." I encourage you to give your children the great gift of their dreams. I have encouraged you to rekindle your dreams, so that your children experience the grace of seeing fulfillment in action. The life lessons I learned in my own early childhood still strengthen and compel me today.

I came face-to-face with injustice in the very first grade. I was six years old, attending Anderson Park School in Atlanta. As much as a little girl can, I looked forward to the excitement of book learning and new knowledge.

I learned to read at home when I was four. I loved reading big books about kings and queens, and the circus, and farms, and outer space. I expected that school would provide me more of the same—only bigger, better, and more serious. My mother was a teacher and my father was an avid reader, so books were an important part of our family life.

The day I arrived in Miss O'Neil's first-grade class, I was ready to immediately receive shiny new books with big words. I secretly expected that I would be able to read to the other children. I knew that most of the kids I'd be in school with couldn't read yet. First grade was when *they* would learn. Since I already knew how to read, I would be ahead of the game. But I expected that my classmates would catch up quickly, and I was willing to help them. Sure, there would be lunch and recess and arithmetic and music once in a while. But mostly school was for reading, and I imagined that our days learning words and understanding stories would be wonderful and full of new knowledge.

Several weeks went by, and our class did not see the first new book, despite the promise of "any day" from dear Miss O'Neil. With no books for each one of us to look at individually, to hold on our desks, to lay our little hands across, the words Miss O'Neil was writing on the board were, to say the least, disappointing. "See Dick and Jane run." "See Spot run." I could care less about that darn dog!

To make matters worse, my desk didn't fit me. I was a small child, and it was just too big for me. Because my legs didn't reach the floor, they would fall asleep, just hanging there. Our whole class was full of hodgepodge furniture. Some of the furniture wasn't even level, including my desk. When I shifted to make my legs feel better, the desk would rock and make a noise. Miss O'Neil would admonish me: "Glenda, stop fidgeting. Glenda, sit still."

Frustration and disappointment got the better of me. The desk wobbled; we had no books. The longer we waited for our books, the worse I felt about school.

Then one morning, books finally appeared. Looking back on that day now, it's almost miraculous how much I remember. I was wearing my brown dress and matching sweater with the rooster appliqué on the collar that my grandmother had sent from South Carolina. To this day I can remember where and how I sat—at a teetering, oversized desk and chair, short brown legs dangling. Waiting, *truly* excited.

"Boys and girls," Miss O'Neil announced, with strained enthusiasm. "I'm going to pass out reading books this morning. I know some of you have been waiting. Well, I have been waiting too, and now we've finally got some."

Miss O'Neil walked down the neat rows of desks, handing a book to each student. I craned my neck to see what was being given out. I couldn't see much, but I felt pretty sure, even before Miss O'Neil got to me, that what I expected was not going to happen. From the way the kids held the books, I could tell they weren't the heavy miracles I'd been looking forward to. In fact, the books looked pretty puny.

As Miss O'Neil got closer to my row, flashing what looked to be a forced smile my way, I could see that these weren't new books at all! The books were used, dirty, wrinkled, and some didn't even have covers!

I felt sure there was some mistake. First graders got *big* books. New books. Our books would take lots of careful creasing and pressing down on the left-hand side to get them to lay flat, to stay open.

After Miss O'Neil had passed out books to everyone, she asked us to open them and start reading in turn. Miss O'Neil called on pupils up and down the rows, asking each to read a few lines. "Pat has a hat." "See Spot run." When it came to my turn, I flushed with panic. The page I should have been reading from was torn out. Ripped right off, so you couldn't even guess what it should say. Miss O'Neil explained that it was no problem and moved on to the next child in my row. *She skipped right over me.* Instead of being able to show how able I was, I was silenced by the damaged book.

We Don't Always Get What We Expect

I was devastated. Here I was, a strong reader able to leap bounds over Dick and Jane. I had missed my turn because these new books weren't new.

When the bell rang, I let my friends—Pam, Beverly, and Maxine—walk home without me. I stayed behind and waited respectfully for the classroom to empty. Then I walked confidently up to Miss O'Neil's desk. She saw me coming, and I imagine she knew exactly what I wanted to say. In my mind there was nothing to feel timid about—I had a problem and she had the answer.

"Yes, Glenda," said Miss O'Neil warmly as I approached her desk. "Do you have something you'd like to ask me, dear?" After all these years, I can still hear her familiar southern drawl.

"Yes, ma'am," I said, "I'd like to know, please, what happened to the new books we were supposed to get? Ma'am, the books you passed out today aren't new at all! The book I got is broken and nasty and I don't even want to put it in my new book bag!"

I took a breath, planning to say more, but mercifully, Miss O'Neil interrupted me. "You're right, Glenda. You're absolutely right. But you're not the only one. As you saw today, no one got new books. And none of the students in the other classes got new books either."

God love her, Miss O'Neil was offering up what she believed would be an explanation I would accept. *Not just me, but everyone.* But I was not in the least satisfied. To tell the truth, I didn't care what anybody else had or didn't have. My love of community hadn't developed yet; my only concern at that moment was for myself.

So, with a child's conviction that wishing makes it so, I repeated, "But ma'am, I just want a new book with big words that I can read out loud to everybody, because I'm in first grade now!"

In my mind, Miss O'Neil had defaulted on her promise. Hadn't she said we'd get *new* books?

Miss O'Neil could see that her explanation wasn't enough for the eager six-year-old standing by her desk. I was not budging from my spot until I got a response that made sense or, better, until I got a new book. Miss O'Neil took a breath. Then she spoke the truth *she* faced: "Glenda, colored children don't get new schoolbooks."

Even as a child, I could see this wasn't easy for her. Saying this to a six-year-old was as hard, probably, as the patch of Georgia clay that substituted for a playground outside our classroom.

"I'm so sorry, Glenda," she continued. "There's not much I can do. But remember, tomorrow is music class, so bring your most beautiful voice with you, and I'll see you in the morning."

I left Miss O'Neil's room in a hurry. Once outside, I began to run as fast as I could, little legs pumping as my plaid book bag bounced against my back. I wanted to find Daddy.

Daddy was my hero then, and he still is my hero. At six, I really believed that Daddy could fix anything. And so I went to find the man who could change my world, who could return my experience of first grade to a time of new pages, new words, and a chance for me to read more and read strong. I really thought that if I could just get home and get him back to the school before Miss O'Neil left, I would get a new book. I remember this so clearly: I thought surely Daddy could and would fix this situation.

Because my parents could not find reliable day care that they could afford, they made a decision—and a sacrifice. Dad took a night job, so that he would be able to be home to care for my younger brother and me when I arrived home from school. When my mother got home, he would take a short nap, and then go to work himself. This is how they managed when we were young, although I understood little about that then, of course. I only knew that Daddy would be at home, and I was glad.

"Daddy, Daddy!" I called as I burst, breathless, into the house. Dad was folding laundry on the kitchen table, his books pushed to the side.

He asked about my day, expecting good news from his "favorite" first grader, and I told him how terrible school had been. I was racing a mile a minute, trying to explain my problem. My despair had stolen my usual coherence. Dad tried to slow me down so he could find out exactly what was going on. All I could do was continue my tiny tirade, talking faster and pulling on his arm.

"Please, Daddy, get up and come with me right now. They close the school soon and you have to talk to Miss O'Neil today!"

"But why, Glenda? What on earth is wrong? Did you get in trouble? Did someone hurt you in school?"

"No, sir. But we got our books and mine was torn and nasty and you have to talk to Teacher, so I can get a new one! You have to help me, Daddy. Teacher says colored children don't get new books, but I know she's wrong. Come on, Daddy, let's go to school!"

"Glenda, stop talking for a minute and listen. Your Miss O'Neil is right. There are no new schoolbooks for colored children. I know it's not fair, but that's the way it is."

My lower lip started to quiver. Once Daddy said something, I might not like it, but even at six years old I knew it was the absolute truth. Daddy sat me down at the table and looked at me in that calm, listen-to-me-now-because-I-can-help way of his and said, "Glenda, I want you to go to your room and take out some of those nice new crayons and paper. I want you to write your own story. It'll be your very own story, with all the big words you know. Go ahead now. Write your own story, the kind of story you want to find in a book all your own."

Dutifully I went to my room, tears sliding down my cheeks. Even my hero, Daddy, had been unable to fix this situation for me. I had no idea that by sending me to create "a story of my own" he was starting an important lesson, teaching me to toughen up. He was giving me an assignment of dutiful thinking and imagination. He was training me to start thinking about building my own future.

Overcoming Obstacles

I sat at my little table and reached for my box of crayons. I drew, and wrote the words I knew, even though I didn't exactly understand the lesson. I was honestly confused, and still crying. I did what my father told me—because we did exactly what our parents said. I did not get the full lesson at that early age. But believe me when I tell you, I have the lesson now.

What I know now, that I didn't know and couldn't know then, is that the pathetic pile of books Miss O'Neil passed out had come through an "unofficial" system of distributing school resources in Atlanta. It's almost inconceivable how consistent and "acceptable" this gross injustice was, but this is how the annual distribution of books was handled. At the end of the school year, white schools threw out their damaged books, to make room for new books that would be arriving for the next school year. The discarded old books were placed on the school's loading dock after the schools were closed for the year, where they sat until schools opened again the following September. At the start of the new year, maintenance workers were sent to pick up the books off the loading docks to be used by students in colored schools across town. By the time we received the books, unforgiving heat and summer rains had sometimes swollen and mildewed the pages or blurred the print.

Books assigned to us were just plain *throwaways*. The teachers— bless their hearts—felt no urgency to obtain this used, damaged cargo.

Now, looking back through adult eyes, I can see Miss O'Neil's bravery and pride. Of course, I realize she probably never made a promise that we'd have *new* books. She would have known better. She would have undertaken the task of sorting and salvaging every year. Some of the books were held together with masking tape. The teachers matched pages and covers, and tried to reassemble books from the scraps they received. Miss O'Neil was surely involved in that, since I clearly remember the taped and raggedy books as I looked around my class.

Sometimes we had to slide our desks over to share books with our neighbor, because, like on my first day, some of us would find that our books did not have the page we read from. In retrospect, I can see how ridiculous and uncaring an educational "strategy" this was.

These were, of course, segregated school districts. All the other teachers in our districts—including my mother, who taught third grade—had the same challenges. They had the same discarded books to make do with. Looking back, I credit myself for being expectant and brave as a child. I would have encouraged and expected my sons to be just like me—to want and to expect the best. Hopefully, each teacher had one or two hungry learners like me, who were disappointed enough and aware enough to ask for an explanation, children who knew the difference between salvage and starting fresh, and who had courage and language enough to dare to ask important questions.

The Supreme Court struck down racial segregation in *Brown v. Board of Education* before I started first grade. But as critical as the ruling was, the landmark decision did not usher in rapid change. The change took time to trickle down and adjust our opportunities as early learners. Our first-grade reading books were not instantly replaced. At our little segregated school—and probably at many others in the South—we remained locked in the grip of Jim Crow long after *Brown v. Board*. Our education, and the plans for our education, continued to be as separate and as unequal as ever. The deliberate and unfair continuation of Jim Crow meant that black schools had to make do with books and furniture that for white schools were trash.

Nobody in the school system saw any problem just dumping their discards onto the outside loading docks. Allowing the Negro janitors from segregated schools to deliver discards was considered doing enough for the colored children across town. Even our crayons were nubbed, collected in a big vegetable can from the cafeteria. We'd have to peel the paper back to use them.

My dear father, miracle worker that he proved to be time and time again, in his wisdom knew that he could not fix a racist society or a segregated school system. He could not give all of us new books, nor could he provide the original covers, nor replace missing pages. He couldn't change the ill-fitting desks or provide playground equipment. He could not fix the ills of the world. But what he could do, and did do, was to strengthen me and help me see in time that the book of life is going to be filled with worn pages and torn pages. Daddy taught me that this is when we must create *pages of our own making.*

When we don't get what we expect, when we are forced to work with less than adequate resources—that's when we must reach deep and pull from the substance of our own souls. Daddy was insistent, very early in my life, that I experience writing a new story, that I learn to come up with my story, on my own.

Later I came to understand that my father was helping me begin to see that disappointment is an obstacle, not a destination, not a place to stop, to spend time, to linger. The segregated, skewed world around me was sending me one message about the lack of equipment and stolen opportunity I would face repeatedly. But my parents—Dad *and*

Mom—were telling me something else. My parents believed that I, a little colored girl from Georgia, could overcome obstacles by the work of my own hands. They said this to me more times than I could count: I could be an architect, a lawyer, an engineer, a doctor. Our parents' mantra for me and my two younger brothers was that we could be *anything in the world* we wanted to be.

I learned as I grew older that racism, sexism, and unfairness exist in this world, and that I could anticipate encountering these slights now and then. I came to see that I *could* respond by standing in front of folk and wailing about being a victim. *Or* I could dare to make a different choice, every time I had a choice to make. What I chose to do, how I chose to respond, was up to me.

The times I describe are history today. *Brown v. Board* has long been the law of the land. But inequalities remain. Consider the state of our current public school systems, supported by property taxes in many parts of the country. Some students get more, some get less. Distribution of educational resources still has embedded inequities. Do our children expect any different now? Are our young learners as hungry? Do we have enough heroes to sit the children down, from day one, and tell them, *No matter what happens, you're in charge. Dare pick up this crayon, and draw the picture you want to see. Dare take this pencil, and write the story you want to read.*

Do we give our children the all-important sense of power and creativity that they will need, and that they can use, every day of their lives?

Miss O'Neil probably felt terrible on that September day, and on many other September days during the many years she endured, trying to teach without adequate material support. Much as I wanted her to, Miss O'Neil could not deliver my dream. Guess what? *Nobody can deliver my dream but me.* If we handle our experiences as lessons, we have an opportunity to get the knowledge we need, to deliver our dreams for ourselves, to ourselves.

In the story I write for myself, I am not trying to fit myself into a new book, or a torn book. Instead, I see myself in the center of a scenario of my own creation. I can use words I have learned, and write the story I dream of for myself. The story I write is by definition a new story, a story uniquely mine, a story that conforms to my personality and my gifts.

We don't get this whole lesson at the age of six, or at our first encounter with unfairness and disappointment. But the lessons we learn the most from in life do begin early. The important lessons we have to learn are reinforced through experience after experience. We can shape new opportunities at every juncture in our lives, if we dare to stop wailing long enough to start working.

Thank goodness, and thank God, for my father's hard work and creative outlook. He was truly a man who understood that hard work can, as the old spiritual says, *make a way out of no way.* My father taught me a lesson that September day that I carried the rest of my life—when confronted with a problem, I should sit down, consider, and write my own story.

First grade—with its wall of segregation and its unanticipated absence of books—did not start me off in school as I had hoped. But lack of resources has not stopped us in hundreds of years, and did not stop me as a young child.

Decades after my despair in first grade, Miss O'Neil was in the audience on the day I was sworn in as judge of the Fulton County Juvenile Court. I kept in touch with her over the years and I made sure she was with me as I took the oath of office. The little colored girl in her first-grade class who was not timid about demanding what she thought was right was still pushing, still striving, still demanding.

I trust that Miss O'Neil was able to see that I hadn't been deterred by what I didn't have. No torn, used, discarded schoolbook, even at the start of life, had power enough to keep me from my goal, which was to read! And now, decades later, look at the irony: I have become both a lawyer and a judge, and this is my second published book.

If in the process of writing our own stories we were to list the names of heroes and sheroes who rose from a state of denial and lack—well, we'd need a lot of time to write. We'd need encyclopedias to list all their names. We'd get lost in the stories of the many who managed to make a difference in spite of struggle. Great achievers learn to motivate themselves, and they learn how to handle struggle. Trials do not deter heroes, even as they honor and respond to what they are motivated themselves to do.

We want to be inspired, but we also want to move beyond others' stories, great that they may be. We want to find the energy and apply the imagination, the mental work, to move our own lives forward.

What we want and need to do is to realize that we have power over ourselves. From early childhood forward, we have control, and we can choose options that will help us create the truth we are seeking.

We *will* be disappointed in this life—by what we don't have, by what we didn't get, by what we wanted versus what shows up. But if we sit down, get still, and think our own thoughts, we can write our own stories, and make heroes and sheroes of ourselves.

Not too long ago, I gave an acceptance speech for the YWCA Woman of the Year award. There was an older woman in the audience, who listened to me recount the story I just told—of the ratty schoolbooks and of my disappointment in first grade. Her name is Mrs. Geneva McCall, bless her heart. Mrs. Geneva McCall, my church member, is retired but spent her whole professional life teaching schoolchildren. She understood and identified with the story I told. A few weeks after that talk, I received a package and a lovely note, in schoolteacher's hand, from Mrs. McCall. The package contained an *absolutely* pristine copy of the mauled reader we used in first grade. Her inscription read, "Dearest Glenda, After all these years, you finally have a new book!"

Taking Charge

My father's life lesson about writing my own story is not just about what happened to me when I was in first grade. My father taught me about taking charge. Even at that young age, he did not want me to create a personal pity party. He did not encourage me to feel sorry over situations that were beyond my control. I needed to learn to control what I could, and control that to the best of my ability. It was a valuable life lesson from a very wise man. I could not and would not be a victim. Writing your own story is uniquely personal, and requires deep soul-searching. The challenge is not to literally write your story (unless you want to), but rather to dare to take charge of the situations that life presents.

You may be a single mother who is struggling to find your way. You have to write your own story, your own plan that will help you not only survive but thrive and soar. A plan to get your child into day care while you further your education. A strategy to save enough money to buy a modest duplex where you can live and earn rental income from the second unit. You may have lost your job during a downturn in the economy, and so you now have to write your own story to use your expertise to start your home-based business, or a cyber-business where you conduct transactions 24/7 all across the globe.

Whatever your story, it is uniquely yours. Do not let other people write your story for you. Others may write that because you are a single mother with minimal resources you will be stuck in poverty for the rest of your life. Or they may write that because you lost your job you could never be competitive in a global economy.

Your story is yours to construct. Dare to take charge. Dare to write your own story.

Today:

Acknowledge that today represents a new chapter in your life. Acknowledge that you are the author of your own story. In one sentence write down one positive thing you want said about your life today!

Dare To:

Write the story of your life the way you want it to be.

- Pick up a pen, now, today, and take the time to sketch the life you want.
- Be brief, but be clear. Write a blueprint, not a book (unless you want to write a book!).

Follow the blueprint you have set out in the story you wrote.

- Use the gifts you have been blessed with.
- Define your own destiny, as you take charge of your own world.

Be the author of your life.

- Be constantly on the lookout for small and large ways you can move yourself toward the story you want to be yours.
- Remember that every story has an author, and you must be the author of your own life.

Conclusion
You're in Charge

I hope you have learned the principles of daring to take charge of your life. I hope you have recharged, reset, or recalibrated your life. I hope you have surprised yourself with the questions you dared to ask, the answers you dared to face, and most important, with the work you dared to do.

I hope you have taken a journey marked by joy and optimism, using the power of your thoughts, using your clarity of purpose, and undertaking a consistent sequence of steps in your own interest, every day. I hope you have used your Joy Journal to make a record of your life-changing ideas.

Let me ask you: Have you jump-started your pursuit of new goals? Have you revitalized old goals and prior passions? Are you reaching, in some way, every day?

Your life is in your hands. You are in charge. You are the compass that steers the ship you're in. You are the main person who has to enjoy and benefit from the way you spend your life. Be sure you spend your life with hope and expectation; be sure you spend your life doing as much as you are able *that is what you* want *to do.* Be careful to keep your spirits hopeful and your actions positive. Dare to expect good, and good will come.

> I believe the most important single thing, beyond discipline
> and creativity, is daring to dare.
> —Maya Angelou

I hope you have benefited from the many stories I've told. Every one of us knows the adage "no pain, no gain." Well, the adage is true, but what is also true is this: we can use our minds and our perceptions to learn from others—from their successes and their mistakes. This is the reason I have told you so many stories. Because there are folks achieving great successes, and making huge mistakes, every day. Why not learn from the textbook God laid out for us? Let's every one of us make only new mistakes.

There is nothing I can do—as teacher, friend, mentor, sister, mother, daughter, judge—to spare you or me from pain in this life. Just as I have, you will have your share of pain. But we don't have to suffer for want of information. We don't have to fail because we can't see how to succeed. Every one of us can learn the strategies that make for success. We can understand from our lives and from others' what works and what doesn't. We can all observe grace, and beauty, and intelligence, and faithfulness, and determination, and devotion, and excellence. We can study the positive with the same intensity as we show when we struggle with disgrace and despair.

Dare yourself to take charge. Live your life on purpose.

Devote today to something so daring even you can't believe you're doing it.

—Oprah Winfrey

Push yourself to *take action*, at all times—*on the positive front.* Do as I say to some of my younger audiences. When you are confronted with the negative, let that drag-down stuff talk to your hand. Say "no" to anything or anyone negative, especially your own negative thoughts. Speak to the negative you encounter in this life: *I don't have time for this, I'm too busy working on my dream.*

Decide which of your dreams are most important to you. Act according to your dreams, in some way, every day. Remember that even if you have plans and dreams for others—like your children—the only work you can truly guarantee is work on your own life. Do not allow your dreams to go silent. Give yourself the same gift you got at birth: exercise your heart and soul and mind and body together, to make of your life the very best life you can.

Live a Life True to You

Dare to ask yourself important questions, even if they're hard. Before and after everything important you do, interview *you.* Ask yourself before you start:

- What does doing my best at this look like?

And after you're done, ask yourself, every time:

- Did I do my best at what I just finished?
- When or if I do that again, how can I do better?
- What will my best look like the next time I try?

One of the world's most famous poets and playwrights, William Shakespeare, wrote centuries ago, "Action is eloquence." If you want to live an eloquent, elegant, true-to-you life, you have no choice but to take action. You take action every day when you go to work or don't, when you are sad or happy, when you eat or restrain yourself, when you exercise or elect not to, when you vote or do not, when you scold your children or hug them, when you call your parents or worry about them, when you save money or spend what you have, when you tithe or do not, when you balance your checkbook or do not, when you take your nephew out to play baseball or choose to ignore his games, when you see your niece on the weekend or forget her birthday, when you go to the grocery store or stop for fast food. When you are elegant, you make a choice. When you are careless, you do the same.

You have the dreams you have because your dreams are waiting for you to reach for them. There's a dream with your name on it—probably more than one. Don't you want to get started? Don't you want to act now?

Dare to make the choices that it takes to win big dreams. Every journey starts with one step. Every accomplishment requires one action to start. Every action depends on one choice.

Every time you make one good choice, or take one useful action, you have one less positive action or one less helpful choice to make on your way to achieving your dreams. Go ahead, dare to be strong. Don't sell yourself short.

I speak to you from knowing, and I speak to you from my heart. Dare to be who you are destined to be. Dare to do what your dreams demand. Take action now, and later, and every single day. Your dreams will come within reach. You will ultimately achieve them. You will be so proud of you. And so will I.

Closing Action:

Remember at the end of chapter 2 I asked you to post your boldest dream? Now that you have concluded this book I challenge you, in fact I dare you, to take charge: to invest an hour and write out a clear plan to obtain what you have dreamed about. You don't want to look back at this point in your life and wish that you had figured out how to claim your boldest dream. Sit down. Think. Write. Plan. Do the very best you can.

Dare to Dream!
Dare to Claim Your Dream!
Dare to Live Your Life on Purpose!

Remember:

Dreams
Are
Realities
Every day

About the Author

GLENDA HATCHETT presides over the two-time Emmy-nominated syndicated show *Judge Hatchett* (Sony Pictures Television).

After graduating from Emory University School of Law and completing a coveted clerkship in the U.S. federal courts, she accepted a position at Delta Air Lines as a senior attorney, litigating cases in federal courts throughout the country. She also served as manager of public relations, supervising global crisis management and media relations for all of Europe, Asia, and the United States. She made the difficult decision to leave Delta Air Lines in order to accept an appointment as chief presiding judge of the Fulton County, Georgia, Juvenile Court.

A graduate of Mount Holyoke College, Judge Hatchett has been recognized as a distinguished alumna by both Mount Holyoke and Emory University. She has previously served on the board of directors of Gap, Inc., the Hospital Corporation of America (HCA), and the Service Master Company. Presently she is a board member of the Atlanta Falcons football organization and serves on the board of advisers for Play Pumps International. In addition, she serves on the Boys and Girls Clubs of America national board of governors. She is the mother of two sons.

Online, Judge Hatchett operates a global social networking site for parents and influencers of children called parentpowernow.com, as well as her personal website, glendahatchett.com, where she can be contacted at Dare@glendahatchett.com.

Follow Judge Glenda Hatchett at www.facebook.com/judge glendahatchett and www.twitter.com/glendahatchett.